W9-CRA-254

Helping Your Child Learn Right from Wrong

A GUIDE TO VALUES CLARIFICATION

by
Dr. Sidney B. Simon
and
Sally Wendkos Olds

McGraw-Hill Book Company
New York   St. Louis   San Francisco   Bogota   Düsseldorf
Madrid   Mexico   Montreal   Panama   Paris
São Paulo   Tokyo   Toronto

Copyright © 1976 by Sidney B. Simon and Sally Wendkos Olds. All rights reserved. Printed in the United States of America. No part of this publication may be reproduced, stored in a retrieval system, or transmitted, in any form or by any means, electronic, mechanical, photocopying, recording, or otherwise, without the prior written permission of the copyright holder.

Reprinted by arrangement with Simon and Schuster

First McGraw-Hill Paperback Edition, 1977

4 5 6 7 8 9 0 BKPBKP 8 5 4 3 2

Library of Congress Cataloging in Publication Data

Simon, Sidney B
  Helping your child learn right from wrong.

  Includes index.
  1. Children—Conduct of life. 2. Moral education (Elementary) I. Olds, Sally Wendkos, joint author. II. Title.
BJ1631.S47 1977   170'.202'22   77–6631

ISBN 0–07–057459–6 pbk.

Marcia Brehmer
Please Return

Helping Your Child
Learn
Right from Wrong

ACKNOWLEDGMENTS

The authors of a book like this are indebted to innumerable people —the families, friends and colleagues who have contributed both to our own personal values searches and to the movement of Values Clarification. It would be impossible to acknowledge by name all who have helped us, but we want to give special thanks to these few.

First, to Louis Raths, whose theory and early pioneering work made this book possible. To Howard Kirschenbaum and Merrill Harmin, fellow toilers in the field of values. To Nora Salaway, who incorporated the search for values into her own and her family's lives and then brought the two authors of this book together. To Jane Stenger, gifted teacher, wife, and mother, who read parts of our manuscript and enriched it with her thoughtful comments. To Barbara Wyden, our talented editor, who helped us shape a philosophy and a collection of strategies into a practical reference for parents. And to the originators of the following values exercises who graciously permitted us to adapt them and include them in this book: Allen Ivey ("If I Were a Book"), Robert Howard and Westinghouse Learning Corporation ("No Red Carnation"), Jane Stenger ("Yesterday, Today, and Tomorrow"), Dr. Thomas N. Turner ("Support"), Robert Siroka ("People in My World"), Rabbi Dov Peretz Elkins ("Religious Unfinished Sentences"), Steve Barish ("Sports Worksheet," "Sports Situations"), and Barbara Glaser-Kirschenbaum ("Family Voting About Male/Female Roles").

We also want to thank the publishers of Dr. Simon's previous books, which helped to lay the groundwork for this one: Charles E. Merrill Publishing Co. (*Values and Teaching*, 1966), Hart Publishing Co. (*Values Clarification*, 1972), and Argus Communications (*Meeting Yourself Halfway*, 1974).

SIDNEY B. SIMON
SALLY WENDKOS OLDS

To these cherished partners in the quest for values,
David, Dorie, Jenny and Nancy Olds
and
John, Douglas, Julianna and Matthew Simon

Contents

CONTENTS

Introduction

Most responsible parents want their children to develop strong bodies and strong minds, and they are willing to spend time with them in activities that will foster such development. This book will convince such parents, as it did me, that we are still neglecting our children.

Often parents are all but leaving to chance a very significant area of their children's growth and development. We are failing to help children find *who they are* and *what they believe and value*. Sidney Simon and Sally Olds, the authors of this important book, greatly expand current notions of what it takes to be an effective parent.

More than that, they will make you realize what you are missing in your family life. From the many exercises and examples of family interaction in these pages, the reader cannot help getting the feeling that family life could be so much more fun, more intimate, more exciting.

It is quite difficult for parents to enter the inner world of the child, and harder still for children to understand their parents. The generation gap does exist in most families, as it always has. Now, for the first time within the covers of a single volume, parents are provided scores of activities (games, if you will) that will bridge the gap between children and adults. These creative games, some simple and some more complex, offer the family the unique opportunity of discovering what all of its members have in common: their human-ness. Parents and children now can get to know each other at a deep and meaningful level—how they think, what they feel, what is important to them, where they are troubled or confused.

When kids are given the opportunity in structured activities to talk about what is *real* and *important* in their lives, they really get turned on. How we adults have underestimated children and youth! Is it not because family life so seldom includes genuine participative activities that would enable parents to observe children's independent thinking, their problem-solving skills, their strong need for autonomy, their logic?

Helping Your Child Learn Right from Wrong provides a new and enriched definition of "family living." It shows us that parent–child alienation need not be inevitable. Coming closer together through sharing core issues and problems common to both parents and children can be the norm, rather than their gradually drifting apart and becoming strangers in the same household. Yet clearly, it will not just happen. Parents will have to make it happen. I know of no better way than using the strategies and procedures tested and proved over the years by the authors. Parents will have to find the time, but this book offers the vehicles.

Probably the concern most frequently expressed by the thousands of parents in my Parent Effectiveness Training courses is "We don't know how to teach our children our own values." Their lack of success in influencing their children's values comes about because these parents almost universally are relying upon methods that are ineffective: they preach, they lecture, they moralize, they shame and blame, they threaten, or they punish. Such methods have a high probability of causing children to resist parental influence and rebel against their parents' values.

In this book, however, the authors offer parents a more effective approach for dealing with complex values issues within the family. Their approach relies on methods that foster a climate within the family in which certain important processes will take place: values clarification, development of self-responsibility for one's values, sharing through two-way communication, development of respect for the values of others, examining options, participative problem-solving. When processes occur in families, values collisions are much more likely to be identified and resolved. Equally important, both parents and children can become what they are capable of being, and they can relate to each other with feelings of mutual respect and love.

DR. THOMAS GORDON
Founder, Parent Effectiveness Training

PART ONE

1

WHO NEEDS VALUES?

Amy, 6, often visits old Mrs. Maloney down the street, who always has home-baked cookies for her. On Halloween, her older cousin Brad, whom Amy adores, asks her to tell him where the old woman lives. Brad says he wants to go trick-or-treating to her house, but Amy thinks he wants to play a trick on her. Should she give Brad Mrs. Maloney's address?

Charlie, 8, has just been invited to join a club made up of boys he has been wanting to be friends with. When he asks whether his best friend, David, can be included, the club leaders tell him that they would ask David if he didn't smell so bad. What should Charlie do?

Ellie, 11, knows that her friend Florrie stole a record from the school's music room. Florrie's parents cannot afford to buy the record and she wants to practice playing her flute with it so she can play in the school concert. Ellen hears that a bully who terrorizes the younger children is being blamed for the theft. Should she speak up? To whom?

Children face conflicts like these every day. Day in and day out, children have to make decisions on the kinds of issues that have engaged the minds of the world's greatest philosophers. But too many children (and adults as well) do not know what to do or how to think when faced by a values conflict. They have no way of evaluating different values systems. They may have superficially absorbed what they have heard from their parents, but they have not built an underlying structure of values to base their actions on. Such children are not sure what life is all about, what the purpose is for their own lives, and what is worth trying to achieve. What are these children like?

Gerry is apathetic. She goes along taking the path of least resistance, since she feels that no value is better than any other.

Harry jumps from one belief to another. On Monday he believes one thing, on Tuesday the opposite; he has no strong anchor in his life.

Irene agonizes over every decision. No matter what she decides, she is sure it is wrong, because she has no firm ground on which to base her decisions.

Jackie is always "in Rome, doing as the Romans." He goes along with his companions in any activity they suggest, from singing in the church choir to shoplifting.

Kate can't agree with anyone. Since she can always find some argument against any value, she is always ready to argue with whatever anyone else believes in; her only value is the opposite from whomever she is with at the moment.

Lawrence is always playing a role. One day he is Honesty personified; the next day, he will do anything to "take care of Number One."

Why is this? Why aren't these children's parents teaching them right from wrong? Giving them guidelines for life? Parents try. Parents have always tried. But what was once relatively clear is now impossibly murky. Which values should we live by? Cooperation and concern for others are good—but so are independent initiative and enlightened self-interest. All of us recognize some absolute values—yet my list of absolute values differs from my neighbor's.

Even when we believe in something, we are not always sure of how to act upon those beliefs. Even when we are sure of our own values, we cannot isolate our children from the rest of the world. Their lives inevitably become more complex as they encounter other people, different experiences, and new ideas. They think. They change. They grow. They begin to question parental values. And we adults question our own values.

Since values are constantly changing, the intelligent person is likely to change attitudes and opinions many times in the course of a lifetime. If we teach children our present values, what do we do two, five, or eight years from now when we hold other values? Say that we taught them false values, that they must now throw them out and learn new ones? No, we cannot.

But we can give them something better. We can give them a system that they can use to arrive at their own values. Even young children can apply this system to their everyday lives. Amy can use it to help her decide whether she should tell her cousin where Mrs. Maloney lives. Charlie can use it to decide whether or not to accept the club's invitation, and what to say to David. Ellen can use it to decide whether to speak to Florrie, to go to the school principal—or to do nothing. This system is what this book is all about.

2

THE THREE MISLEADING M'S

Up to now, most parents have relied on what we call "The Three Misleading M's"—Moralizing, Manipulating, and Modeling—to instill values in their children. As we shall explain, these are no longer valid teaching tools.

MORALIZING

Father tells Mark, "It's your duty to study hard in school. You owe it to us, after all we've done for you."

Mother tells Nancy, "Don't you know that stealing is a sin? God doesn't like thieves."

Whenever parents invoke religion, patriotism, or emotions (like guilt) to transmit their values to their children, they are moralizing. Moralizing has certain advantages. It certainly lets children know where their parents stand on specific issues, and it provides a standard to measure their attitudes by. It is a quick and efficient way to communicate beliefs, and it can be used with all the children in a family.

But moralizing can be a dangerous roadblock to genuine communication. It implies that your children's concerns are not as important as yours. It is hard to keep from looking shocked and horrified when your children say or do things that disagree with your opinions, when those opinions have been

18

stated in a moralizing atmosphere. The critical tone that accompanies moralizing makes children feel they are being personally attacked.

Moralizing is also confusing. Children in our society get many conflicting messages—even at home, since both parents cannot agree absolutely about everything. When the differing messages from teachers, clergy, friends, popular heroes, radio, and television are taken into account, we can see how difficult it is for children to form their values on the basis of moralizing alone.

MANIPULATING

Mother asks Patsy, "Do you want to wear your red skirt or your blue one?"

Richard knows he will receive a dollar if he brings home a report card with all A's.

Stephen gets punished when he hits his little sister—if his parents find out.

Father asks Rachel, "What would the neighbors say if they saw you in that see-through blouse? They would think we were terrible parents to let you run around like that."

Limiting our children's options to those that we can readily accept, providing them with a spurious choice in which one alternative is clearly unacceptable, controlling them with rewards and punishments, appealing to their love for us are all forms of manipulation.

Some arguments can be made for manipulating children. Encouraging small children to make limited choices does give them practice in choosing and does give them some sense of their own power in controlling certain aspects of their lives. Rewards and punishments do encourage children to behave in certain ways, and there are instances when, for the good of the child and the rest of the family, behavior must be controlled. Appealing to their love for us does make them think about the ways their actions affect other people.

But there is one basic flaw. Manipulated children are not learning how to think through conflicts; how to weigh pros and cons, how to decide issues on their merits. Instead, they are learning to solve their problems on the basis of extraneous issues—such as how much they care about hurting other people's feelings or how much they want a reward or fear a punishment.

Manipulation often invites ugly power struggles, as children in turn find ways to manipulate parents. In the struggle they are diverted from their real task in life—learning how to direct their own lives.

MODELING

Some parents try to teach values by setting a good example. Father feels that if he is industrious and thrifty, the children will learn from what they observe. Mother tells the story about George Washington and the cherry tree to impress upon them the importance of telling the truth, and she makes special efforts not to lie in front of them.

There is a lot to be said for modeling. Psychologists have found that the behavior of others *is* a powerful influence upon the way children act. They are more liable to be aggressive if they view a respected adult acting in an aggressive way; they are more likely to settle disputes amicably if they have seen others doing the same. Children of alcoholics are more likely to grow up to become alcoholics; children of smokers are more likely to smoke. Young people tend to do what we do, not what we say. They are quick to spot inconsistencies between our words and our actions. Conscientious parents want to close the gap between their words and their deeds, so they can present congruent models to their children.

But being human—and thus less than perfect—parents do not always set the ideal example. Dad tells Oliver to be honest —and then he lies about the boy's age so he can pay half-fare on the train. Mother preaches the importance of self-control— and then she goes on a binge eating chocolate-chip cookies.

How can children know which parental behaviors they should copy and which they should disregard?

Furthermore, parents are not their children's only models. Whom should they model themselves after: Mother, Father, older brothers and sisters (and which ones)? Their clergyman, teacher, scout leader, gym coach, or best friend? The top hitter on their favorite baseball team? The star of their favorite television program? The President of the United States? Each is a model for children. Each reflects a different value system. Whose example would you want *your* child to follow in every situation?

Through the centuries, there have always been parents who avoided the whole issue. There still are. Father tells Ted, "I realize that no one value system is right for everyone. What right do I have to impose my values on you? You just figure things out for yourself and do what you think best, and I won't try to influence you in any way. You'll just have to learn how to make up your own mind." This laissez-faire approach is really a form of modeling: these parents set an example of not committing themselves. Children rightly interpret such a lack of parental involvement in their lives as a lack of caring. They learn a values lesson—not to commit themselves to anything.

Father was not being honest with Ted. It is impossible to be neutral about values. Our children pick up the way we feel by the things we say and the things we do—and by the relationship between the two. When we do nothing about an issue, they get the message that this is something we don't care about. We are constantly giving messages to our children, and we need to be clear about what these messages are.

WHY THE THREE MISLEADING M'S
DON'T WORK ANYMORE

At one time or another, these three approaches may be desirable. Sometimes we do want to advance our reasons and display our emotions to inspire our children. Certainly we want to set good examples for them. We often want to limit young children's available choices to those that are wise and safe and healthy. When certain behaviors are very much prized or deplored, rewards and punishments may be indicated. In situations that are well within a child's ability to handle, we may want to stay out of the picture entirely.

But as useful as these approaches may be in raising children, none of them teaches anything about values. None helps children learn to analyze confusing ideas and situations, and to decide what to do. Young people need help in deciding important issues. Without guidance, they are like a pilot without a control panel. They do not have enough experience to weigh alternatives or to foresee consequences.

So what are parents to do?

For years, many parents have intuitively helped children to work out their own values. Within the past several years, many more parents have turned to the Values Clarification system. This approach has helped thousands of parents help their children. The following chapter explains how Values Clarification works.

3

SEVEN STEPS TO VALUES

Values cannot be taught. But the process for arriving at them can be. We *can* teach our children to examine life rationally, to understand that they usually have a range of possible decisions, to consider the consequences of those decisions, and to make their choices based on their awareness of the options and the consequences. Then we can help them learn how to scrutinize their lives to see whether they really are living according to what they say they value. We can impress upon them the importance of arriving at their own personal values—not impulsively, thoughtlessly, or under the influence of others—but through deliberate consideration.

How can we do all of this? Through the process of Values Clarification. This approach helps us to examine our own values and help our children to examine theirs. It does not promote a single values standard, but rather teaches an individual how to go about determining just what values to believe in.

As we help our children establish their values, we have to think about our own. And as we do, we will undoubtedly discover that we are becoming clearer about what we ourselves believe in. We will probably also find that some of our values are changing as we ourselves change and grow.

Twenty years ago, the senior author of this book was doing his graduate studies in education with Professor Louis Raths at New York University, who had long been observing the ways people come to feel that certain beliefs and actions are right or wrong. The old simplistic morality, Professor Raths believed, did not explain the difference between the ways that people actually think and act—and the ways they think they should think and act.

After years of observation, Professor Raths concluded that people arrive at their true inner values only after taking seven arduous steps. These seven steps, which are described as the seven rungs on the ladder to values, constitute the basic process of Values Clarification.

Let us depart here from the third person as I, Sidney Simon, tell you, the reader, how working and studying with Professor Raths made me think more and more about my own values. I became absorbed in analyzing the way I was leading my life. And, as a result, my entire life changed. My thinking about values penetrated all my teaching, to such an extent that I stopped teaching subject matter as such. As an English and social studies teacher, I now was finding less meaning in the history of a war or the structure of a sonnet, and more meaning in the search to find value in life. I became so convinced of the need to spread this philosophy to others that I became a missionary and made time in my schedule for more speaking engagements and more in-service workshops.

One experience in particular exemplifies the way my new thinking changed my life. As a professor of education at Temple University, I had been teaching my students, future teachers, that grading was a pernicious academic institution. I had also been teaching the necessity of acting upon one's beliefs. Yet I was, in accordance with university policy, still giving grades to my students. I decided that acting upon my values meant that I had to stop giving grades. This decision would have, I knew, serious professional consequences. It did. Temple denied me tenure. But I was sure I was right.

Others thought so, too. My students sponsored rallies in my behalf. Prominent fellow educators spoke in support of my stand. The Philadelphia newspapers wrote about me as a "mild-mannered, gentle professor" who had jumped into a raging storm of moral controversy. Finally, Temple University reversed its decision and granted me tenure. I felt vindicated not only by this decision, but also by the offer that came—and that

I accepted—a year later, when the University of Massachusetts asked me to be part of its exciting new Center for Humanistic Education. Here I have been ever since, free to teach for the joy of teaching and free to further develop the values-oriented philosophy that has come to guide my life.

THE SEVEN STEPS TO VALUES

Each one of the seven rungs on the ladder to values is a *value-indicator*. A value-indicator is a belief, an opinion, an attitude, an interest, or an isolated act—anything that lets us know that we are in the process of forming a value. A *value* is a principle by which we lead our lives. Not until a person has rigorously followed up his or her value-indicators by completing all seven steps can that individual say that she or he truly knows and is living by a set of values.

These seven steps are demanding criteria. Often, when people start to analyze their values—or those beliefs they had always thought of as values—they realize that, according to these standards, they have very few true values, just value-*indicators*.

As an example, how do you, the reader, feel about smoking cigarettes? Many of us are confused about smoking. Mother feels she shouldn't smoke, but she does. Father stops smoking but resents depriving himself of something that relaxes him. The teenager who for years begged her parents to stop smoking is now lighting up regularly herself. Some parents puff away as they tell their children, "Don't start. You'll just get hooked like me."

The Seven Steps fall into three major categories: Choosing, Cherishing, Acting. Each category represents a plateau.

First Plateau: Choosing Beliefs and Behaviors

1. OPTION EXPLORATION: WHAT CAN I DO?

What are your alternatives? You cannot be said to hold a value if you had no real choice in the matter or if you were not aware of the possible choices. You have to decide deliberately, instead of drifting unthinkingly into action or inaction. You have to know what options are available, and you have to check them all out.

If you just drifted into smoking because everyone else was doing it (in other words, if you never considered options other than the one you took), you have not explored your options. Smoking options might include:

a) Smoking as much as you want to
b) Limiting yourself to a pack a day
c) Postponing your first cigarette of the day till after lunch
d) Not smoking yourself, but not trying to influence others
e) Expressing disapproval to those you love, but not to outsiders
f) Discouraging all other people from smoking in your presence

2. *CONSEQUENCE COUNT:* *WHAT WILL HAPPEN IF . . .?*

Your choice is an informed one if you make it not impulsively or emotionally, but only after careful thought about possible effects. Most courses of action carry a combination of favorable and unfavorable results, which then have to be weighed before you decide.

Your thinking about the consequences of smoking might go something like this: "If I smoke heavily, I am more likely to get lung cancer, emphysema, and a heart attack; my breath will smell bad; I may burn holes in clothing and furniture; and I will be spending X dollars every week on cigarettes. But I will have a satisfying way to discharge nervous energy and maybe I'll save money that otherwise I'd be spending on psychotherapy. (At this point, you may swing back to Step 1 to consider other possible options. For instance, can you think of other ways than smoking to alleviate nervousness? Add them to your options list.)

"If I limit myself, I am less likely to contract a smoking-related disease. If I don't smoke at all, I am least likely to. If I give up smoking, I might gain weight, and that's a health hazard, too. Which is the bigger risk?

"If I don't smoke but permit others to do it in my home, I

may still suffer from the smoke in the air. If I ask my guests not to smoke, I may cut down physical risks, but I will risk losing those friends to whom smoking is very important."

Which consequences are most important to you?

3. *FREE CHOICE: DO I REALLY WANT IT?*

Your are choosing freely if you have not been coerced or pressured, if you are not looking for a reward, avoiding punishment, or worrying about what other people will say or do.

If you don't smoke because your doctor said cigarettes would kill you within the year, because you don't have enough money, or because you are afraid your parents will punish you, you are not acting freely. If you do smoke because that's the "cool" thing in your crowd, then you are still not choosing freely, but are acting according to what other people want. Your choice is free only if you have come to it after rational thought about all the basic options and their consequences.

Second Plateau: Cherishing Beliefs and Behaviors

4. *ACCENT ON THE POSITIVE:*
AM I HAPPY AND PROUD ABOUT IT?

You are really happy about your choice. You have not made it on a negative basis, but have made a positive selection you feel good about.

If you keep saying, "When I'm 65, I'll start smoking again because then I won't worry about my health," you show that you consider your choice the lesser of two evils. But if you say, "I'm so glad I don't smoke because I feel better, I'm not tied to a habit, my food tastes better, and I'm not polluting the atmosphere," then you are happy and proud about your choice.

5. *ROOFTOP SHOUT:*
DO I LET THE WORLD KNOW ABOUT IT?

Since your are proud of your choice, you want to tell everyone about it. You take every opportunity to let others know your decision.

You could decide not to smoke yourself but not say anything to other people for fear of sounding like a "do-gooder." (Al-

though why this has become a "dirty" word, we don't know—
we still prefer it to doing bad!) But if your opposition to smoking is a real value, you will need to broadcast your belief. You
could write letters to magazines urging them not to carry cigarette advertising. You could wear an anti-smoking button or
attach a bumper sticker to your car. You could decline cigarettes by saying, "No, thanks. I don't believe in smoking." No
one will have any doubts about where you stand on this issue.

Third Plateau: Acting upon Beliefs
6. *VALUES ACTION: WHAT CAN I DO ABOUT IT?*

You go out of your way to translate your beliefs into action.
You spend time, energy, and money to support your value. In
regard to smoking, you can get rid of all your ashtrays, put up a
sign asking visitors not to smoke in your home, join an anti-
smoking organization, lobby for no-smoking sections in public
places, and ask smokers to put out their cigarettes in no-smoking areas—even if it sometimes involves an ugly response from
the smokers.

7. *PATTERN-BUILDING:*
WHAT CAN I DO—AND DO—AND DO?

When you have a value, you do not act on it once and then
forget it. Your actions become a regular pattern in your life.

If you write one letter to the editor but no more, if you wear
your anti-smoking button once and put it away, if you ask one
person not to smoke in an elevator and decide you've done
your bit, then you are not acting consistently over time. But if
you continually seek out ways to implement your anti-smoking
value, and if you incorporate these ways into the pattern of your
daily life, then you are carrying out this final step in the process
of valuing.

WHAT ARE MY VALUES?

Most of us hold very few values that would meet all seven of
these criteria. But very often, a little more thought and a little

more action can turn a value-indicator into a value—and give us one more guidepost to a richer life.

Here is one homely example of a value that both authors of this book have incorporated into their lives. Both of us live in communities where we do a fair amount of shopping in large shopping centers with huge parking lots. We each make a trip to one of these centers at least once a week. The first question we face when we go to the center is where to park. We can apply the Seven Steps to this one simple decision, as follows:

1. Option Exploration: I can try to park as close as possible to the store I'm going to; I can park at the farthest end of the lot; or I can park anywhere in between.

2. Consequence Count: If I try to park close by, I'll have to circle through the lanes, wait for people to pull out, and run the risk of a fender-bender accident, but once I park I'll be able to run quickly into the store. If I park at the farthest end of the parking lot, I'll save time by being able to park immediately; I'll be able to remember where I left the car; I'll get exercise walking from the car and back to it.

3. Free Choice: No one is coercing me one way or the other.

4. Accent on the Positive: I feel good about coming to a sensible decision about this frequent activity, and I like my reasons for my decision to park at the farthest end of the lot.

5. Rooftop Shout: When the supermarket helper asks me, "Couldn't you find a closer parking space?" I say, "Yes, but I like to park at the far end." I tell him why.

6. Values Action: The parking is the action.

7. Pattern-Building: I park this way every time I go to a shopping center.

Our lives are made up of one small decision after another. When we give thought to our everyday decisions, we can invest them with more meaning and we can better integrate them into our overall values system. So in this one instance, by thinking seriously about as mundane a matter as where we park our car to shop, we can foster our values of saving time and getting exercise. More important is the thinking itself. When we pay attention to the small decisions, we are better equipped to make the large ones. We are on our way to constructing value-filled lives.

This is the way one family applied the Seven Steps to Values to solve conflicts over the weekly marketing trip. They turned it into a planned family outing. Everyone went, and before going, everyone went over the list.

Katie, 8, asked if each child could choose one item at every shopping expedition: one cereal, box of cookies, or kind of fruit. After discussion, the family agreed that everyone's item would have to be placed on the list ahead of time, to prevent impulse buying. To avoid waste, no one would be allowed to buy a new cereal or a new box of cookies if the previous one had not been finished. This plan follows all of the Seven Steps to Values:

1. Option Exploration: Before putting an item on the list, each person thought about all the things she or he might choose.

2. Consequence Count: Everyone knew that she or he couldn't get certain items the next week if this week's purchase was not eaten.

3. Free Choice: No one tried to influence anyone else on the one item; all were free to make up their own minds.

4. Accent on the Positive: Everyone felt good that this approach was a good solution to what had been a constant source of conflict.

5. Rooftop Shout: When the family was in the store, people around them could hear them discussing the items each had chosen.

6. Values Action: The marketing was carried out according to plan.

7. Pattern-Building: The plan was followed every week.

Not all decisions lend themselves to this kind of analysis. Many values come about indirectly as the result of Values Clarification strategies, explained in the next chapter.

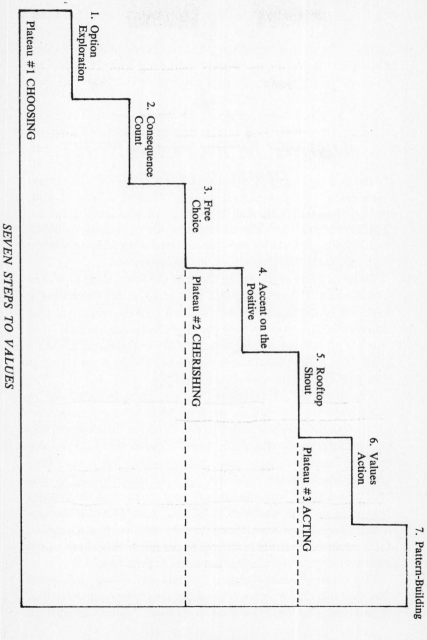

SEVEN STEPS TO VALUES

1. Option Exploration
2. Consequence Count
3. Free Choice
4. Accent on the Positive
5. Rooftop Shout
6. Values Action
7. Pattern-Building

Plateau #1 CHOOSING
Plateau #2 CHERISHING
Plateau #3 ACTING

4

USING STRATEGIES TO FIND VALUES

The Seven Steps to Values constitute a way to analyze beliefs and attitudes, but taking these seven steps is an arduous process that requires commitment, time, and intelligence.

One can think of the Seven Steps as the foundation of Values Clarification. The structure that is built upon this foundation is made up of strategies. Webster's Third New International Dictionary defines "strategy" as "a careful plan or method" and "the art of devising or employing plans or stratagems toward a goal." The Values Clarification strategies bring people closer to their goal of a highly rewarding way of life.

The strategies are exercises that are concerned with one or more steps in the valuing process. Most of them seem like games, but they are not parlor games—fun for the moment, forgotten immediately afterward; they are games that help individuals and families to raise important issues in a lively way. They get the whole family into the habit of questioning the way people live their lives, the choices they make, and the reasons behind them. The strategies help their users look for the options in any situation and examine the possible consequences of these options. They also help people examine their lives to see whether they really are living according to their beliefs.

By "playing" these "games," people strip away the layers that hide their inner selves from those they love, and even from themselves. Families who have embraced Values Clarification find that the strategies sometimes make this process effortless and occasionally raucously funny. Other times, it is more strenuous and challenging. The only thing it never is is dull.

All the strategies force us to look more closely at ourselves, at the things we love and the things we hate, at what we want out of life and what we're putting into it, at the people we care about and the ones who care about us. The regular use of strategies turns the theory of Values Clarification into a system that can become a treasured part of every family's life.

Dinner-table conversation becomes more than "pass the peas." Rides in the car become more than "when are we gonna get there?" Holidays gain a new richness. Sabbaths become more meaningful. Family members enjoy each other's company more.

In the course of the senior author's work as a teacher of teachers, he began to use the handful of strategies first conceived by Professor Raths. As he taught, as he worked with his colleagues, and as he raised his own family, he devised more and more strategies. The thousands of teachers who have made Values Clarification part of their classroom practices find that new strategies constantly suggest themselves. This system continues to grow and to meet the ever-changing needs of the individual, the family, the group. Parents and children who start out by using the strategies in this book will undoubtedly find that they want to adapt some of them to make them more meaningful. Eventually, they will be developing their own strategies.

Let us take a look at one of the strategies.

Strategy 1

MY FAVORITE THINGS

The world is so full of a number of things
I'm sure we should all be as happy as kings.
—ROBERT LOUIS STEVENSON
A Child's Garden of Verses

Have you ever thought about all the things in this world that make you happy? All the things you really get great joy out of doing? Most people who do this strategy are surprised to discover how many things give them pleasure. In a group, you see many smiles as people write down some of their pleasurable activities. Some are as simple as taking shoes off at the end of the day or watching a cat walk sideways.

Before people can enjoy this strategy fully, they need reassurance that their lists will be private, and won't have to be shown to anyone.

Like many of the strategies, "My Favorite Things" calls for making a list. Lists often bring you data that you have but that you don't know you have. You can compare yourself to Mr. Brown, who periodically goes to the rear of his general store to count what he has on his shelves. Once Mr. Brown knows his inventory, he can decide what to order and what to mark down. When you know more about yourself, you are better equipped to make decisions about spending your time, energies, and money.

So much of our time is taken up with thinking about the things we *have* to do. The beauty of this strategy is that it forces us to look at the things we really *love* to do. We can't go after what we want until we know what means the most to us. There are no right or wrong answers for what we *should* love to do. The strategy asks only what we really *do* love to do.

Good times to do this strategy are after dinner, or any time the family is all together. This is also fun when guests are present. And it is a real joy on occasions when aunts and uncles, cousins and grandparents get together. The pleasure that family members receive from sharing their favorite things with each other, from getting new views of each other, and from finding common interests becomes like a presence in the room. Any place will do, as long as everyone has a surface to write on. You need pencils and large sheets of paper for everyone. Legal-size lined pads are good.

Step 1. Ask everyone to fold a sheet of paper the long way and to write the numbers 1 through 20 on the left of one of the folded-over sides. Then everybody, including the starter of the strategy, writes down "Twenty Things I Love to Do." The starter should make a point of saying that the things you love to do can be small things or big things—as small as opening the mail or as big as taking a vacation in another country. If people have trouble thinking of things, you can stimulate them by asking them to think about:

- the four seasons and what you like to do in each
- favorite places and what you like to do there
- favorite people and what you like to do with them
- favorite possessions and what activities they represent

For very young children, you might cut the list down to five or ten things. If the children are too young to write, someone can help them. It's all right to put down a couple of extra items or run a couple short.

Step 2. Code your list. This helps you see patterns in the things you love to do and discover the kind of person you are. Unfold the papers and put symbols down opposite your twenty activities. At any one sitting, you will want to use up to five or six codings. Any more than this serves up more information than anyone can digest. At another session, you can use different codings. Here are some good basics for the first time:

$ Beside any activity that costs more than three dollars (or whatever amount you set) every time it is done. Don't count the money it initially cost to buy equipment (like a bicycle, record player or backpack).

A Activities you prefer to do alone.

P Activities you prefer to do with other people.

AP Activities you enjoy equally whether alone or with others.

2 This would not have been on your list two years ago.

M You think this would have been on your mother's list when she was your age.

F Ditto for your father.

When did you last do each activity? You can put down the date or just say "last month, last week, yesterday, today," etc.

Circle the five activities that are most important to you, and then rank them from 1 to 5 in the order of their importance.

Right after doing this strategy, the members of one family had some "Ah-hah!" experiences (see Strategy 2, page 49). Annie, 16, said, "I always thought I wasn't at all materialistic, but I learned that it takes a lot of money to make me happy." Billy, 8, said, "I was surprised to find out that practically everything I like to do has to be done with somebody else." Their father added, "I decided I have to re-order my life, because I'm not doing enough of the things I really love."

This strategy, like most of the others, can be expanded, varied, and followed up in many ways, as you'll learn in Chapter 7. But before doing any of the other strategies, read the guidelines in the next two chapters. With an understanding of how best to start, your experiences with the strategies will be more meaningful. You may want to re-do this and other strategies from time to time, to see how your values are changing.

5

FOURTEEN GUIDELINES FOR PARENTS

"If you were to be born with a great gift, which would you prefer—a beautiful singing voice, great athletic ability, or skill with your hands? Rank your choices in order." (See page 56.)

"Do you think cheating is ever justified?" (See page 64.)

"Are you more like a rose or a daisy?" (See page 53.)

These three questions are all from the first group of Starter Strategies (page 46), search-launchers to help people discover what they value. Many of the questions in these and other strategies sound unrelated to values issues, and more entertaining than educational. Many others deal with issues so deep that they are rarely discussed even in the bosom of the family, sometimes not even between husband and wife. Light or heavy, all the strategies have three parts.

First, they *elicit a response* related to a values issue.

Second, the strategy starter (who may be any family member, even the youngest) *accepts all statements in a non-judgmental way.*

Third, all the people taking part *look at the data* generated by the strategy with an eye to the Seven Steps to Values.

The strategies are best handled informally, as just one more family discussion. But for maximum effectiveness, the starter should keep these three parts in mind.

To get the most out of the strategies, parents should get together before introducing them to the children, and should agree to abide by the fourteen guidelines outlined in this chapter.

When we talk about parents, though, we realize that an increasing number have to do the job of both father and mother. One out of every ten children in the United States is growing up in a home with only one parent. These parents have a demanding job, and it is remarkable how well so many of them cope all by themselves with all the responsibilities of bringing up children.

One of the weightiest of these responsibilities involves helping children work through values-related conflicts and decisions. As we have pointed out, it is hard enough to do this when there are two adults who can provide support and encouragement to each other in helping their children deal with difficult, emotion-laden issues. The single parent often feels most alone in carrying out these important tasks of parenthood.

Single parents who have adopted the Values Clarification approach have found it particularly helpful. Neither the basic structure, the Seven Steps to Values, nor the strategies require two parents working together. In fact, the emphasis on finding one's own answers is appreciated especially in those families separated by divorce, when one of the major problems is a basic difference in values between the two parents. With Values Clarification, there is no need to pronounce one parent right and the other wrong. Nor is there any pressure on the parents to agree.

For some of the strategies, small single-parent families may want to get together with friends or relatives, but this is a matter of individual choice.

The guidelines below have evolved from the experiences of thousands of families who have made Values Clarification work for them.

1. ACKNOWLEDGE YOUR OWN CONTINUING SEARCH FOR VALUES.

You don't have to be or act all-knowing just because you are a parent. You know you don't have all the answers to life. No one does. Yet many of us feel that we have to pretend that we do. We often act this way out of a mistaken belief that we are thus providing security for them. But it is a false security, a crutch. An all-knowing attitude on the part of parents prevents closeness within the family. It aggravates the children's feelings of powerlessness and inferiority. It keeps families from learning and growing together. Worst of all, it is dishonest. The search for values is one we pursue as long as we live.

2. BE OPEN AND FORTHRIGHT IN STATING YOUR OWN BELIEFS.

Most of us have strong feelings about many value-related issues. We want to let our children know how we feel. And we *should* let them know. We owe it to them to explain our feelings and to illuminate the thinking behind them, to let them know that our values—and our value-indicators—are important to us.

3. DO NOT ASK FOR OR EXPECT AGREEMENT FROM ANYONE ELSE.

You have every right to feel whatever way you do. So has everyone else. Those values we consider basic and even absolute may be so for us. But they may not be so for all people at all times. And that includes our children. They are not extensions of us—but separate feeling, thinking human beings.

4. LET THE CHILDREN EXPRESS THEIR POINTS OF VIEW BEFORE YOU EXPRESS YOURS.

Our children are influenced by the way we think—and by the way they think we want them to think. If you are a person of strong convictions and if you express these first before your children get a chance to express theirs, they may be reluctant to be honest. They may even shift their opinions after hearing yours, and you may never know what they really thought. They themselves may never know.

5. BE SHOCK-PROOF.

No matter what your children (or your spouse or any other participant) may say, don't express horror, disgust, or strong disapproval. If you start to moralize, you'll lose their interest and participation. Children sometimes give "shocking" responses initially to test the safety they have been promised. When they see it is really there, they are more genuine.

6. USE ONLY ONE STRATEGY AT A SESSION.

Don't crowd a session. Even if a particular strategy misfires and doesn't seem to arouse much interest, don't say to yourself desperately, "What else can we try to save the session?" You have plenty of time for trying out other strategies. Even if there isn't much immediate response, a strategy may still have made a strong impact. The whole family or just one member may well go on thinking about the issues raised.

7. KEEP YOUR SENSE OF HUMOR.

These discussions should never be preachy, stuffy, and humorless.

8. DON'T PUSH TOO HARD.

Keep the session at a level your family finds comfortable, whether it's every day, three times a week, or once a week. Whatever is comfortable and fruitful and fun is right for your family. Be flexible, too. If a big event comes up on a Values Clarification night, don't worry about shifting, or even skipping, the discussion. Values Clarification can fit into your life comfortably on either a regular or an occasional basis.

9. BEGIN WITH ISSUES ABOUT WHICH YOU DON'T HAVE VERY STRONG FEELINGS.

This way, you'll be less likely to moralize, judge, get excited, or persuade. After everyone has become more comfortable with the process of valuing, tackle the weightier issues. But if you have to work hard right at the beginning to bite back anger or sharp disagreement, you won't enjoy the strategies—and neither will anyone else in the family.

10. RAISE ONLY THOSE ISSUES THAT YOU THINK YOUR CHILDREN ARE OLD ENOUGH TO MAKE JUDGMENTS ON.

Try to use the kind of language and specific situations that even the youngest can understand. But don't be afraid occasionally to tackle an issue that's pertinent only to the older children.

11. USE THIS BOOK AS A GUIDE, NOT A BIBLE.

We suggest a great many strategies here, provide examples, and suggest ways of doing them. We do this basing our recommendations on our experiences in the more than fifteen years we have been using Values Clarification strategies in our own families and in the classroom, in the workshops we have been leading for the past ten years, and on the experiences of other families. We have given considerable thought to these strategies, and most of them have been tested and found successful. This does not mean, though, that every one will work for your family. What may apply perfectly to your next-door neighbors may seem strained or artificial around your dinner table.

So use only those strategies you feel comfortable with. They are your tools, not your handcuffs. Adapt them to make them more meaningful. Make up new ones. Always cast them into your own language and experience, and use examples that your family can relate to.

12. DO NOT USE VALUES CLARIFICATION TO MANIPULATE YOUR CHILDREN.

There are times when Values Clarification is not appropriate for discussing a topic or a course of action. When this is so, do not try to cloak your decision in the trappings of the strategies. Do not try to give your children the illusion that decisions are theirs when they are not. Do not try to bring them around to your point of view during a values discussion. Do not ask questions for which you have an answer in mind.

When you find out that Peter stole a dollar from Ronnie's wallet, you would not ask him, "How would you feel if I did that to you?" You would not ask other questions that would make him defensive. You might use clarifying responses instead (see page 157) and ask, "What else could you have done?" "Where else could you have gotten the money you needed?" or "Was it very important to you to have an extra dollar?" You would let Peter know that his action was wrong, but you could also use the opportunity to help him examine the thinking that led to his unacceptable behavior.

13. *PLAN YOUR VALUES CLARIFICATION SESSIONS.*

Schedule sessions when the family can be together, undistracted, with plenty of time. One good time for many families is at the dinner table, after the main-course dishes have been cleared away and before dessert is served. Others prefer to set aside a time over the weekend. Others keep a list of strategies in the glove compartment of their car, to pull out for long rides.

Take the telephone off the hook.

Do some thinking ahead of time about the strategy you plan to use.

14. *THE STARTER OF THE STRATEGY ALWAYS PARTICIPATES.*

It is essential that whoever starts a strategy participate fully. This makes for a joint search for values. Even if you have already done a strategy that the rest of the family is doing for the first time, you will benefit from doing it again.

Once you have decided to try this new approach with your family and have discussed the Fourteen Guidelines, you can launch your family's search for values. The next chapter will help.

6

SEVEN GROUND RULES ⨍ FOR EVERYONE

Now you are ready to begin.

You can start using the strategies in a number of ways. For example, simply say one night at dinner, "Let's talk about everyone's high point of the day," and ask all family members to share their high points, without specifically identifying this as a High Point "Whip" (see page 51) or as anything different from any other dinner-table conversation.

Or you might prefer to offer some kind of brief introduction. The value of an explanation stems from the fact that some of the principles that are so important in Values Clarification are very different from the ways we typically react to each other. You might say, "We're going to do something that we haven't done before, and we want to ask everyone's cooperation. We think you'll like it. If you do, we can do it again another time." Then you could briefly spell out the following ground rules:

1. NO ONE JUMPS ON ANYONE ELSE.

This is a time for total acceptance of other points of view. Once all family members have spoken, people may express personal disagreement—but never in a judgmental, or "put-down" manner.

2. THERE ARE NO "RIGHT" OR "WRONG" ANSWERS, ATTITUDES, OR RESPONSES.

Whatever way a person feels is valid for that individual. You might feel differently in a similar situation, but that does not deny the reality of the other person's feelings. With behavior there *are* rights and wrongs—we simply cannot allow people to harm themselves or others. But we cannot and don't want to control the ways people of any age think and feel.

3. *ONLY ONE PERSON TALKS AT A TIME, AND NOBODY INTERRUPTS*.

When we are listened to with warmth and attentiveness, we know we really matter. Interrupting makes the speaker lose his or her train of thought and feel as if what he or she has to say isn't important. It's distracting to listeners, too, since interruptions take a conversation all over the place, instead of allowing it to remain focused. The rest of us lose out when we hear only a fragment of what the speaker wants to express.

4. *EVERYONE HAS THE OPTION OF "PASSING" AT ANY TIME*.

You always have the right to decline to answer any question. The Values Clarification body language for this is to fold the arms across the chest and say, "I pass." No one tries to coax, wheedle, or put any pressure on someone who wants to pass. This important safeguard lets all family members retain their privacy and not reveal more than they feel comfortable about.

5. *NO "KILLER STATEMENTS" THAT PUT DOWN OTHER PEOPLE*.

When people express their own feelings or the way they might have reacted to a situation, they need to avoid criticizing or ridiculing someone else. No one is called a dummy, a fool, a doormat, a hypocrite, a prude, a thief, or any other derogatory label.

6. *NO SELF-PUT-DOWNS*.

The minute someone starts to say, "Boy, was I a dope for doing that . . ." or, "I never do anything right," or some other self-denigrating comment, the other members of the family should remind the speaker that Values Clarification builds us up; it doesn't let us tear ourselves down. (More about this in Chapter 10, I Am Lovable and Capable.)

7. *CHANGING ONE'S MIND IS A SIGN OF GROWTH.*

Instead of ridiculing each other for inconsistency when someone says something at odds with a previous statement or action, we learn to rejoice in each other's growth.

Now then, you have prepared yourself. You have prepared your family. You are ready for the Starter Strategies.

7

STARTER STRATEGIES

The following strategies are good introductions to this new way of family communication. Start with any one you like, stick with it as long as your family seems to get something from it, and then go on to another. Don't feel you have to do all the strategies in this group before going on to another group. Just do what seems right and comfortable. That's what Values Clarification is all about.

THE STARTER STRATEGIES

1. My Favorite Things
2. Ah-hah!
3. The Whip
4. The Seesaw
5. Priorities
6. Values Spectrum
7. Family Voting

8. Provocative Questions
9. Magic Boxes
10. Dreams Can Come True
11. Who Am I?
12. Lifeline
13. Lucky Thirteen
14. When We Were Very Young

Strategy 1

MY FAVORITE THINGS

There were thirteen around the dinner table that hot August evening—the junior author, her husband, and their three children; and the children's grandparents, aunt, uncle, and two cousins. We all did "My Favorite Things." Tears came to my eyes as I learned that my father's list included "going shopping for my wife." After fifty-five years of marriage, he still gets joy from buying my mother gifts! I had to laugh when I found that another of his entries involved taking her to a baseball game. Wishful thinking. He's never gotten her into the stadium yet, but at 75, he's not about to stop trying. My 17-year-old niece and I were delighted—and amazed—to find that we had both put "holding babies" on our lists. We squeezed each other in our new common bond.

Each of us learned something about ourselves that evening. But the overwhelming sense of that hour or so was the deeper understanding we developed as we learned new things about each other. At the end of that visit, we knew each other a little bit better, we respected each other's uniqueness, and we felt a new closeness as a family.

"My Favorite Things" is a versatile strategy. Some families enrich their experience by doing variations of it every couple of months and comparing their lists each time. It can be varied by changing the coding as follows:

L Activities that you need lessons to enjoy fully.

D You have to drive or be driven to do this.

Pl Planning is required (making an appointment, buying a ticket, etc.).

R An element of risk (physical, emotional, or intellectual) is attached.

I Involves intimacy with another person.

IQ You'd enjoy it more if you were smarter.

Ath You'd enjoy it more if you were more athletic.

Y You'd enjoy it more if you were younger.

O You'd enjoy it more if you were older.

Ch You hope your own children will have this on their lists some day.

Mo You hope to be doing more of this.

5 You think this will *not* be on your list five years from now.

B You'd like to become better at it.

"My Favorite Things" can also be varied by changing the emphasis. For instance, ask people to write down "Twenty Things I Love to Do . . ."

- on a rainy day (good for days when the kids ask, "What can I do?")
- on school holidays (ditto)
- with my family (good for planning family activities)
- alone (good on days when "there's nobody to play with")
- with my best friend
- in school or at work
- that don't use gas or electricity (good to combine with a discussion on energy conservation)
- that don't cost any money
- that you can still do with your leg in a cast (done by one young athlete who broke her leg at the beginning of what was going to be a very energetic summer)
- on weekends
- with my hands

Or ask everyone to write down "Twenty Things I *Don't* Like to Do" (coding could revolve around ways to make them better, other activities that could be substituted for them, benefits you get from them even if you don't like them, etc.).

FOLLOW-UP: Here are three activities that some families like to do after the basic strategy. You can probably think of more.

1. Ask everyone to talk for two minutes about one item from their list. They pick any activity they want, or they're given a choice of two (by picking either activity #3 or #12 on their list, for example), or they talk about one of their top five. The talk might take one of these forms:

   - Simple facts—when you like to do the activity, with whom, and under what circumstances.
   - Why you like it—what pleasures and satisfactions it gives you.
   - Your ideal version of the activity. For bicycle riding, you might describe the ideal weather, companion, destination, clothing, sights, and so forth.

2. Follow this strategy immediately with Strategy 2: Ah-hah! (See below.)
3. Toss out questions like the following (they may be answered out loud or in the privacy of everyone's own mind):

· Are you the kind of person who actively plans your life? Or do you just take whatever comes along?
· Are you willing to take risks?
· Do you know your parents well? Would you like to know them better? How could you make this happen?
· Do you need a lot of money to make you happy?
· Do you need other people to make you happy?
· Are you willing to invest time, energy, and money in lessons and in practice? Do you feel that such efforts to improve yourself will help you get more pleasure out of life?
· Are you in a rut or are you constantly discovering new joys?
· Are you making the most of your mental and physical abilities?
· Are there things on your list that you don't *really* like but that you think you *should* like?

Strategy 2

AH-HAH!

> *Who in the world am I?*
> *Ah, that's the great puzzle!*
> —LEWIS CARROLL
> Alice's Adventures in Wonderland II

Often we don't realize what we have learned from an experience until we have put a thought into words. Then we get an "Ah-hah!" experience such as those described on page 50. When we share our personal insights with others, we share a piece of ourselves. We also inspire others to think in new ways about themselves. This strategy helps us to sum up what we have learned about ourselves from special experiences, like a three-day power failure ("I was happy that we were able to do a lot of things to make up for the electricity we didn't have"), a camping trip ("I was unhappy that there are so many outdoorsy things that I don't know how to do"), or a family crisis ("I never realized before how much I really love Grandma"). It is also a good way to check ourselves periodically, perhaps every evening ("What did I learn about myself today?") or every Sunday ("What did I learn about my life this week?").

GOOD TIMES FOR DOING THIS STRATEGY: Immediately after another strategy; soon after a special experience; every evening; every week on the same day.

GOOD PLACE: Anywhere.

EQUIPMENT NEEDED: None.

PROCEDURE: The starter asks all present to think for a minute or so about what they have learned about themselves, their lives, or their values. Then everyone formulates one of these learnings into a sentence that begins along the lines of the following:

· I learned that I . . .
· I realized that I . . .
· I was happy that I . . .
· I was surprised to find that I . . .
· I was unhappy to realize that I . . .
· I noticed that I . . .
· I have to do something about the fact that I . . .
· I re-learned that I . . .
· I remembered that I . . .
· I never before realized that I . . .
· I found it hard to believe that I . . .
· I felt good that I . . .

The focus of everyone's statement should be on the self. It is so easy to avoid getting to know ourselves by hiding in generalities like "I learned that people. . . ." But the real meaning of these statements lies in what each of us learns about ourselves.

Encourage people to write down as many of these statements as they want, and then invite each person to share one. Everyone has the option of passing. No one's statement is discussed. No one is put in a position of having to defend his or her statement. These statements are considered gifts, given and accepted.

If your family likes to keep journals, you might each write down your statements, date them, and save them. You might also post your statements on a family bulletin board.

After you have done this strategy, you will have given form to your new thinking about yourself. You will have consolidated some patterns in your life and some insights into yourself.

Strategy 3

THE WHIP

"I'm proud," said Carla, 9, "that I stuck up for Debbie when the other kids started being mean to her."

"I'm proud," said Ethan, 12, "that I made the track team."

"I'm proud," said Father, "that I've been doing my exercises every day."

"I'm proud," said Mother, "that I finished the painting I've been working on for so long."

This family was doing "The Whip," a strategy that whips around the table to get everyone's quick answer to one question—in this case, "What did you say or do in the last twenty-four hours that you're proud of?"

TIME: Any time the family is together.
PLACE: Dinner table, car, beach, picnic grounds, anywhere.
EQUIPMENT: None—or a kitchen timer for the follow-up discussion.
PROCEDURE: The starter poses a question, and everyone gives a short answer. The conversation then flows freely, perhaps picking up on the topics raised.

SAMPLE "WHIP" QUESTIONS:

· What was the high point of your day? Of your week?
· What was the low point?
  (Alternative: What kind of day/week is it when you can't think of either a high or a low point?)
· What did you agree with someone about today?
· What did you disagree with someone about?
· What did you say or do in the last week/month that you're proud of?
· What is one thing you have changed your mind about recently?
· What is one thing you'd like to change in your school? Your job? Your neighborhood? Your town? Your country? The world?
· If there were a fire in your home and you could save only one possession, what should it be?
· What made today special for you?
· What part of today would you like to experience tomorrow?
· How did you care for yourself today?
· What did you need today and didn't find?
· Who made the day brighter for you?
· What part of today was hard for you?
· What are you looking forward to tomorrow?
· What is one way you hope your children's world will be different from yours?
· Who is one person you think you can learn something from? What would you like to learn from this person?
· How did you handle a recent disagreement?
· What is something you believe in so strongly that you would risk death?
· What do you think is the biggest problem in the world? What is one thing you think could be done about it?
· What is one thing you'd like to learn before you die?
· Where is the place where you feel safest in this world?
· Who is the person who, more than anyone else, makes you feel good about yourself?

- Where would you love to retire to?
- Who in public life would you like to be like?
- What movie touched you most deeply this year?
- When did you last cry?
- When did you last laugh out loud?
- Where is the most beautiful view you have ever seen?
- What is something you would really love to learn how to do?
- If you could get the President to listen to you, what would you ask him to do?
- What was the best thing you ever did for someone?

FOLLOW-UP: Anyone who wants to discuss his or her answer more fully is allotted a specific amount of time, anywhere from two to five minutes. Thus, Carla could tell about the incident involving Debbie, Ethan could relive his triumphant try-out, Father could explain why he started to do exercises and how he feels after doing them, and Mother could talk about her painting.

This strategy is not just a perker-upper of dinner-table conversation. By focusing on specific aspects of our lives, it brings us information about our feelings and our opinions that we may not have thought about before. It helps us to know ourselves.

Strategy 4

THE SEESAW

The question tossed out at the dinner table was, "Which would you rather be—a daisy or a rose?"

Jennifer, 15, answered quickly. "I'd rather be a daisy. I wouldn't want to have thorns. I don't want to think of myself as staying on the defensive and not letting other people get too close to me."

Dorie, 12, also said, "Daisy . . . because daisies are fresh and like spring." She jumped up from the table, started pantomiming and humming the theme from Beethoven's Ninth Symphony. "But roses are too heavy, too serious."

When Mother's turn came, she chose to be a rose, "Because people are always pulling petals off a daisy, and I wouldn't want to have my petals pulled off."

And Father: "To me, daisies are too lightweight. Me—I'm a rose."

This family was doing "The Seesaw" strategy. Sometimes life is like a seesaw. We can play only by choosing one side or the other. Too often, too many of us try to stay in the middle. But when we avoid choosing sides, nothing happens. We don't accomplish anything, we can't move, and our life comes to a standstill in many important ways. At other times we rush too quickly into taking sides, and we find ourselves flat on the ground or dangling in the air. This entertaining strategy forces us to make a commitment to one of two choices—and then to explain our reasons.

TIME: Any time.

PLACE: Anywhere.

EQUIPMENT: Watch with a second hand or a kitchen timer.

PROCEDURE: The starter asks a "seesaw" question like: "Which are you more like—a river or an ocean?" Everyone gets one minute to answer and explain. The conversation may take off from here to other topics, or a few other questions may be tossed out. Generally, three or four questions are the limit at any one session.

SAMPLE "SEESAW" QUESTIONS:
Are you more like . . .

· the city or the country
· a house or an apartment
· a saver or a spender
· a rose or a daisy
· a lion or a fox
· a dog or a cat

- a cowboy or an Indian
- the driver getting a traffic ticket or the police officer giving it
- a teacher or a student
- David or Goliath
- a leader or a follower
- the heart or the brain
- hot or cold
- a rock band or a symphony orchestra
- a comic book or an encyclopedia
- a TV set or a radio
- a Cadillac or a Volkswagen
- a steak or a hamburger
- a bubbling brook or a placid lake
- champagne or soda pop
- a baseball or a bat
- a tree or a leaf
- a movie star or a senator
- brain or muscles
- a garden or a farm
- a sky diver or a skin diver
- a newspaper or a magazine
- oregano or garlic
- a pizza or a chocolate éclair
- a shoe or a sock
- a blender or a knife sharpener?
- Are you more "yes" or "no"?
- Are you more likely to skate on thin ice or to tiptoe through the tulips?

VARIATION: Family members can look at each other with regard to the characteristics in each question and point out how they see the other members of the family.

"The Seesaw" illustrates the difficulty of making a decision, the necessity to consider various facets, the very personal nature of many of our decisions, the kinds of things that are important to us, how we see ourselves, and how our self-concept influences us.

Strategy 5

PRIORITIES

Most of our decisions are *not* either/or propositions. There are generally many options, and a hard but necessary task is to decide after we have figured out what the possibilities are, in what order they meet our needs.

When we are forced to determine our priorities—to rank our choices in order—we think hard about them and consider the pros and cons of each one. This is an extremely useful technique for solving the conflicts of daily life. You will probably get even more from those questions and possible answers that you make up yourself from current events: family conflicts, hopes, and goals; and priorities that your own family needs to establish.

PLACE: Dinner table, car, beach, living room, back porch, anywhere.

TIME: Any time, but especially when the family has a problem.

EQUIPMENT: Kitchen timer if your family is very talkative.

PROCEDURE: The starter asks a question and provides three or more possible answers. Everyone thinks for about a minute, ranks the answers in order of desirability, and takes a minute or two to explain his or her rankings.

When discussing an actual problem, family members:

1. Brainstorm to come up with all kinds of possible solutions.
2. Eliminate those that are completely unacceptable.
3. Rank the rest in order of desirability.

Many problems that at first seemed insoluble will thus turn out to have a range of more-or-less acceptable solutions.

SAMPLE QUESTIONS:

If you had bad breath, which of these would you prefer?
· your best friend tell you
· receive an anonymous note
· your parents tell you
· nobody tell you, and you wouldn't find out

What do you think our country's biggest problem is?
· poverty
· communism
· pollution
· crime

Where would you most want to live?
· in a two-room apartment on the 28th floor in a low-income housing project
· with four brothers and sisters and your parents in a trailer in a trailer park
· in a suburban housing development where all the houses look alike

Which would you least like to be?
· so poor you didn't have enough to eat every day
· so disfigured that people turned around to stare at you
· so retarded you had to be placed in a special class for slow learners

Where would you most want to live?
· on a farm
· in the suburbs
· in the city

Which punishment would you hate the most?
· to be scolded by a parent in front of one of your friends
· to be spanked
· not to be allowed to watch TV for a week

If you told a friend about a problem of yours, which would you want the most?
· sympathy

- advice
- understanding

If you told a parent about a problem, which of the above would you want?

Which meal would you least want to go without?
- breakfast
- lunch
- dinner

What is the most important thing for parents to give their children?
- independence
- compassion
- motivation to succeed

What would be the most exciting thing that could happen to you when you're 16?
- get your driver's license
- take a trip to Europe with your family
- go steady with someone you really love

When you're not hungry, what would you most hate your parents to say?
- "Think of all the starving people in Africa."
- "If you don't eat your dinner, you can't have dessert."
- "I went to a lot of trouble to cook your favorite foods—and now you don't even eat them."

Would you be most likely to believe something if you . . .
- read it in the newspaper
- read it in a book
- heard it on the radio
- saw film clips on TV
- heard it from your parents
- heard it from your teacher
- heard it from a friend?

Which of these sentences is most important to you?
- I can shape my life.

· I know how to find joy in living.
· I deserve to be happy.

Strategy 6

VALUES SPECTRUM

The Values Spectrum is a good strategy for "compulsive moderates"—people who try to avoid conflict and commitment by straddling every fence they come to. When they do this, of course, they can't get off the fence, can't get onto solid ground, can't get any farther on their journey. On many issues there may be a set number of *actions* we can take, but there is an infinite range of feelings. We can identify with an extreme point of view on one side or on the other. Or we can take a position somewhere in between. This strategy helps us to realize how many different shadings there are on every issue and to share our thinking.

TIME: Any time, but especially when a controversial issue comes up in conversation.
PLACE: Anywhere you can write.
EQUIPMENT: Long sheets of paper and pencils.
PROCEDURE: The starter identifies the issue—say, the wearing of seat belts. The topic may grow out of a family conversation, out of a news item, or from anyone's concern about an issue. With imagination and humor, the starter then identifies two characters at each end of a spectrum based on this issue and writes down their names, connecting them with a line, as in this example:

SCISSORS SOL .   .   .   .   .   DRIVE-IN DAN
hates seat belts so much he loves seat belts so much he
cuts them out of other people's wears them in the drive-in
cars movies

The paper is then passed around the table, so all can put their initials on the point of the spectrum where they feel they belong. Everyone is urged not to choose the exact middle but to commit him/herself to one side or the other. After the paper has gone all around, all the family members tell why they placed themselves where they did. If the issue engages people's interests, a lively discussion should follow.

SAMPLE SPECTRUM ISSUES:

EAT-OFF-THE-FLOOR EDITH . keeps her room so spic and span her floor is cleaner than the kitchen table.

GARBAGE-DUMP GRETA has to wear knee-high boots to wade through all the rubbish and garbage she throws on the floor.

SEX-ROLE SUE . . . . . thinks girls should wear only ruffly dresses and should be helpless and boys should never wash a dish or make a bed.

UNISEX URSULA treats her sons and daughters exactly alike, not telling anyone (even the children themselves) their sex, saying it doesn't matter.

WALKING WALT . . . . has to walk 25 miles to Grandma's house for Christmas dinner and walk back carrying presents.

CAR-SEAT CARL insists that his mother provide taxi service so he can play with the kids next door.

FRUGAL FRED . . . . . weaves the cloth for his own clothing from the cotton he has planted.

SPENDING STEVE buys any clothing he wants anytime he wants it, even though he already has 12 just like it.

LAZY LAURA . . . . . does no chores at all around the house; she hires neighborhood children to do them.

SLAVING SARAH does all the cooking, cleaning, laundry, shopping, while her parents lie in the sun.

DIRTY DOT . . . . . . washes her hair once a year at tax rebate time; if she doesn't

SHAMPOO SHERRY washes her hair every time she combs it.

get a rebate, she puts off the
shampoo till next year.

EARLY ED . . . .
gets to the airport 24 hours
ahead of time with a sleeping
bag to be the first in line at the
check-in counter.

RAMP-RUNNER RODNEY . . . .
gets there just as they're pulling away the ramp.

Discussions on these issues can sometimes be made more interesting by asking such questions as: "Did you feel the same
way last year?" "Do you think you'll always feel this way?"
"What could change your mind?"

These spectrum issues are fun to make up, especially when
they are sparked by issues your family is really dealing with.
By using humor, you can often deflect the angry feelings that
may have grown up around a specific issue.

Strategy 7

FAMILY VOTING

Sometimes the more articulate or the more dominating members
of a family express their opinions freely, while the shyer ones
keep theirs to themselves. This strategy encourages all family
members to express themselves on a variety of issues in an easy,
enjoyable way. In a spirit of fun it points up the wide range of
opinions that can exist within the same family, and it under-
scores the legitimacy of that range. Just because people are
related to each other, live in the same home, and share *some*
values does not mean that they all have to agree on everything.
This strategy helps us see where we agree and where we differ
with each other. The lively discussions it sparks help family
members to appreciate their uniqueness.

TIME: Any time, but especially when family or friends are visiting.

PLACE: Anywhere.

EQUIPMENT: None.

PROCEDURE: The starter explains that the group is to vote on questions as follows:

- If you agree, raise your hand.
- If you agree strongly, wave it in the air.
- If you disagree, point your thumb down.
- If you disagree strongly, move your thumb vigorously back and forth.
- If you want to pass, fold your arms across your chest.
- If you have no feelings on the matter or are not sure, do nothing.

The starter should not overwhelm the group with too many questions—ten to fifteen is a good number. In posing them, gear your questions to those present, taking into account everyone's age and experience. It's a good idea to start out with one or two that are not heavily laden with emotional connotations, before getting into more controversial ones that people might be shyer about answering.

The questions can cover a variety of topics, or they can concentrate on one or two general areas like money, friendship, love, or any of the other ten values-rich areas (see list on page 171).

SAMPLE QUESTIONS:

How many of you . . .

- think children should earn their allowances by working around the house?
- have ever felt lonely even in a crowd of people?
- have had a close friend of another religion?
- have had a close friend of another race?
- are afraid of getting fat?
- regret things that you've done in the past?

- think parents should punish by spanking?
- think a family isn't complete without children?
- think no one should have more than two children?
- have ever cheated on a test?
- would like to be President?
- would like to live in the country?
- like to go to big parties?
- would be willing to donate your body to science?
- like pillow fights?
- would like to do more things with the family?
- think teenagers should go steady?

VARIATION: Take turns asking questions. Everyone asks one or two, or people take turns handling the entire session.

FOLLOW-UP: One of the questions is chosen for discussion, in which people explain why they voted as they did. After the discussion, the question is asked again so that people have the chance to change their answers.

Strategy 8

PROVOCATIVE QUESTIONS

A free-wheeling, unstructured discussion in which everyone has a chance to express his or her opinion; often gets people thinking about questions they never considered before.

TIME: Any time.
PLACE: Anywhere.
EQUIPMENT: None.
PROCEDURE: Starter tosses out a values-oriented question like the ones below to start a talk about the issue involved. The discussion that follows differs from conventional conversations or arguments because it is approached from the viewpoint of the Fourteen Guidelines for Parents and the Seven Ground Rules (see Chapters 5 and 6).

SAMPLE QUESTIONS:

· Are there ever times when { lying, stealing, cheating, killing } is justified?

· What would the world be like without { cars, TV, winter, children, mothers, fathers, grandparents, Christmas, dentists? }

· Whom do you have to say "I'm sorry" to?
· What does this world need that you can bring to it?
· Where are all the places that you feel safe? How can we help you to find more of those around here?
· Pretend that you are twenty years older . . . what would change in your life?
· If you were five years younger, how would you use those five years differently?
· What are some things that take courage?

   The list of questions could go on forever. As you approach more family discussions along these lines, you will probably find that you are making more of an effort to understand each other and to approach issues with fresh eyes.

Strategy 9

MAGIC BOXES

Imagine that a messenger has just come to your door. She tells you that outside in the truck there are three packages for you: a large box, a medium-sized one, and a tiny one. The messenger has orders to put in each box whatever you ask for, and to bring it to you.

What would you want in each box? You can choose something tangible or intangible, realistic or fantastic, silly or serious. The only criterion is that whatever you choose will bring joy to your life.

When the Lee family filled their magic boxes, Grandma put in her tiny box "the engagement ring that I pawned fifty years ago so we could pay the rent," 18-year-old Ted put an acceptance letter from college in his, and Father put in his a photograph of his father, whom he had never seen. Medium-sized boxes held a set of encyclopedias for Mother, a telephone call from a special boy for Karen, and the novel that Father dreamed of writing. Their big boxes were crammed full with such things as a pony, a house by a lake, a trip around the world, and "good health for everyone in the family."

TIME: Any time.

PLACE: Anywhere.

EQUIPMENT: None, or (for variation) three different-sized boxes, and pencils and three pieces of paper for everyone.

PROCEDURE: The starter explains the strategy as in the first two paragraphs above. Everyone takes a couple of minutes to think and then shares his or her answers.

VARIATION: Everyone writes down his or her choices and puts the papers in the appropriate-sized box. All the papers are then read aloud, and people try to guess who said what.

FOLLOW-UP: People are asked:

· What could you do to receive delivery of your three magic boxes? Whom could you ask for help?
· What would you put in for your mother or father? Your husband or wife? Each child in the family? Your best friend? The public person you most admire?
· Think of three items in each category, and then rank them in order according to their importance to you.

Strategy 10

DREAMS CAN COME TRUE

All of us have daydreams in which our lives become just the way we want them to be. Often we can make our daydreams come true. This can happen when they have some link to real life, when we communicate them to people who have the power to change things and the will to express their feelings for us, or when we act upon them ourselves. This strategy encourages us to dream, and then to try to make our dreams come true.

TIME: Any time.
PLACE: Anywhere.
EQUIPMENT: Kitchen timer.
PROCEDURE: The family chooses a topic, such as those listed below. Everyone gets four minutes to describe what would represent perfection within the category. After each person has taken his or her turn, the other family members ask questions focusing on how the speaker's dream can come true.

DESIGN THE PERFECT . . .

vacation	weekend
birthday	dinner
Christmas	sunset
Chanukah	job
summer	parents
school day	school
marriage	evening out
workday	party

QUESTIONS:
· What can you do to make this dream come true?
· Whom can you ask for advice or practical help?

· Do you have the money to do this? If not, how can you earn it?
· What percentage of perfection would you settle for?
· Tell about the most perfect experience in this category so far in your life.

Strategy 11

WHO AM I?

We are more than the face that looks back at us from the mirror every morning, more than the collection of statistics we put down on official forms. Each of us is a fascinating collage of facts and feelings, set in a particular place, a particular time, and a particular set of personal circumstances. Sometimes we don't really know who we are.

Filling out the "Who Am I?" form helps family members focus their pictures of themselves.

TIME: Any time.

PLACE: Anywhere you can write.

EQUIPMENT: If you can make inexpensive photocopies of pages 68 to 70, this would be ideal. Otherwise, large sheets of plain paper will do. Pencils, either way.

PROCEDURE: The starter explains that everyone will be filling out an autobiographical form that will be completely personal and private. No one else will see it. Then the starter passes out either the copies of pages 68 to 70 or the plain sheets of paper. If plain paper is handed out, the starter reads aloud the beginnings of the sentences that people are supposed to complete. Someone volunteers to write down the answers for the youngest children. Anyone can choose to pass on any question, but even if people decide not to put their answers down on paper, they are urged to think about the questions and answer them in their own minds.

WHO AM I?

Date _____

My name is _____.

My address is _____.

I was born on _____, which makes me ___ years old.

My sign of the zodiac is _____.

My social security number is _____.

I have lived in _____ for _____ years. Before

that I lived in _____ different places. They are _____

_____.

I am the _____ (1st, 2nd, 3rd, etc.) child in a family of _____.

I have ___ sister(s) and ___ brother(s).

The chores that I do at home are _____

_____.

The thing my friends like best about me is _____

_____.

I thing the best thing about me is _____.

I think the worst thing about me is _____.

A person I would like to be like is _____

because _____.

The thing I am proudest of having done is _____.

The thing I am most ashamed of is _____.

I am in the _____ grade at _____ School.

My job is _____.

I work for _____.

My favorite $\begin{Bmatrix} \text{boss} \\ \text{teacher} \end{Bmatrix}$ was _____ because _____

_____.

My worst { boss / teacher } was _____ because _____

_____.

The best thing about school/work is _____.

The worst thing about school/work is _____.

If I were a { boss / teacher } I would { act / teach } this way: _____

_____.

On my job / In school } I like best to work (alone, with one other person, with

a group).

My favorite color is _____. This color makes me

think of _____.

My favorite food is _____.

My favorite TV show is _____.

My hobby is _____.

In my free time I like to _____.

Some of the things I don't like are _____.

If I could buy anything I wanted, I would buy _____.

If I could go anywhere in the world, I would go to _____.

If I could do anything I wanted, I would _____.

If I could be any animal for a day, I would be a _____.

I would really like to see _____.

A famous person I would like to meet is _____.

The thing that makes me happiest is _____.

The thing that makes me most unhappy is _____.

If I could have one book, I would like a book about _____

_____, but I would never read a book about _____

_____.

I would like to ask a wise person these questions:

1._____?

2._____?

3._____?

Strategy 12

LIFELINE

An old man lies gravely ill in a hospital. He knows that his life is almost over. He murmurs almost inaudibly, "What does it all mean? What did it all mean?"

None of us should have to wait to ask this question with our last words. All of us should know that we asked this question throughout our lives and struggled with all our might to find our own answers. If we keep trying to make sense out of life, we can bring new wisdom to its chaos and confusion. And we can begin to learn now what life is all about.

This strategy helps both adults and children come to terms with the fact that our years on earth are measured, and that all of us have only a limited amount of time to accomplish what we want with our lives. It is an upbeat way to focus on the way we want to spend that remaining time that we all have.

TIME: Any time the family is together; especially effective with people of different ages.

PLACE: Anywhere you can write.

EQUIPMENT: Large sheets of paper and two different-colored pencils for everyone.

PROCEDURE: With one of the pencils, draw a horizontal line the long way across the paper, representing your life.

Place a dot at each end. The dot on the left represents your birth; write your date of birth above it. The dot on the right represents your death; either estimate a date when you *think* you might die, or put down one which you realistically *hope* you would live to.

Put an X on the line to show where you are right now.

Make marks on the line to indicate some of the most important events in your life up until now. Don't make any suggestions to the children about what they might put down. Their lifelines should represent their own conceptions of what is important in their lives. If they seem stymied, though, you might start them off by suggesting such landmark events as the start of school, the move to a new home, etc.

Use the second-color pencil to make marks on the line to show what you hope to accomplish in the years ahead.

Share your lifelines with each other. Explain your highlights, both those that have already taken place and those that are in the future.

Ask questions like these:

· What is the first thing you can do to make your first projected highlight a reality?
· Is there anyone you can ask for help in this?
· What help do you need from any of us in the family to help you accomplish one of your highlights?
· Do you feel your goals are realistic?
· If you could accomplish only two of your highlights, what would they be?
· Who is someone you think has made a great deal out of his or her life?
· Who is someone you know who has done very little to make very much out of his or her life and who probably will end up like that old man, asking "What does it all mean?"

Setting our lives out on paper like this is a dramatic way to help us see them more clearly, assess what we've done with them in the past, and plan what we want to do with them in the future.

Strategy 13

LUCKY THIRTEEN

From ancient days, "13" has been a magical number. This strategy lets you use its magic to get in closer touch with your values.

TIME: Any time.

PLACE: Anywhere you can write.

EQUIPMENT: Pencils and paper.

PROCEDURE: Everyone writes down thirteen items—maybe thirteen things that are in his or her bedroom. The starter then poses priority questions about the thirteen items, such as: "Which three of these could you give up most easily? Cross them out." "Which five of those that are left could you live without pretty easily? Check them." "Which of the thirteen would you rescue first in case of fire? Draw circles around the three that would be most precious."

The family could then discuss the possibility of acting upon what they have just learned—maybe selling or giving away the three items apiece that people could most easily give up. Don't moralize; don't phrase this as a "should." Just bring up the idea and see how everyone feels about it. This strategy *could* lead to housecleaning, charitable contributions, a profitable yard sale. Or it can be just a recognition of the things everyone treasures.

SAMPLE "13's":

· 13 things around the house that run on electricity, which you personally use. If there were an acute power shortage and you were asked to cut down your use of electricity, which three could you give up most easily? Which would be hardest to give up? Are there any you would want to give up right now to save energy and cut down on the electric bill?

· 13 books that you own that you'd take to a desert island. Which would you take if you were to cut down to three?

· 13 people not in your immediate family whom you like to spend time with. Three whom you wouldn't really miss if they moved away and you never saw them again. Three you'd miss so much you'd move to a different city if you could, to be close to them. Put the date when you last saw each person next to their name.

· 13 toys you like to play with. Three you could give up most easily. Three you want to save and pass on to your own children.

- 13 places where you spend your Saturday afternoons. Three you wouldn't miss if you never went there again. Three you would really miss.

- 13 TV shows you watch sometimes. Three you wouldn't miss if they went off the air. Three you'd miss so much that you'd write to the network to ask that they be put back on.

- 13 things you do in a typical day at school or work. The three you dislike the most. The three that are the best parts of your job or school day. A discussion might follow on changing the worst aspects—how to make them better, how important they are, etc.

- 13 places where you might want to take a vacation sometime. The three you wouldn't care about if you never got there in your whole life. The three that you'll make it your business to get to someday.

- 13 foods you like to eat. The three you'd give up most easily if you had to go on a diet or save money. The three that would be hardest to give up.

- 13 phone calls you want to make. The three that you wouldn't care about if you never made them. The three that you'll definitely make, no matter how many times you have to dial.

- 13 people you'd like to invite to your next birthday party. The three you wouldn't invite if your parents said you could only have ten. The three you *would* invite if you could only have three.

- 13 ways you could save money. The three ways that would be easiest for you. The three that would be the most difficult.

- 13 household chores that family members have to do. The three you dislike the most. The three you like the most.

- 13 articles of clothing. The three that would be the easiest to give away if a poor person came to your door asking for used clothing. The three that you like so much you'd be willing to wash them by hand or pay for their drycleaning out of your allowance if you had to.

Strategy 14

WHEN WE WERE VERY YOUNG

"When I was little I always played in the bathtub with all my toys and stayed in until my fingers were all wrinkled up; I never wanted to get out," reminisces 8-year-old Walter. "There was one special boat I loved that Aunt Ann gave me."

"I remember the feel of that rough washcloth my mother would use to scrub off the dirt," says Mother, as the years disappear, leaving her back in that old claw-footed tub. "I didn't take more than one bath a week and I used to like to play out in the fields behind our house. So I really needed that scrubbing. And oh, how my mother would complain because I didn't like to sit inside and sew like my sister." Mother smiles as she adds, "It wasn't so fashionable to be a tomboy then."

"I remember once when I defecated in the bathtub," recalls Father. "I haven't thought about this in years. I remember, too, the spanking I got. I don't know which I cried harder about— my sore fanny or the shame of having done such a babyish thing. I don't know how old I was, but I know that I was old enough to be ashamed."

Our values do not come full-blown out of the air. We learn them from our early experiences and the reactions of those around us. How have we learned our feelings about cleanliness? How did we get our attitudes about our bodies—how they looked and felt and how safe it was to look at or feel them? What were the special times in our early lives? And what made them special?

Most of us—even young children—love to go back in time to rediscover the little child we once were. This strategy helps us do that.

TIME: Any time.
PLACE: Anywhere.
EQUIPMENT: Kitchen timer.

PROCEDURE: Think back to a time when you were very young—a time before you went to school or your earliest memory of a certain kind (see Sample Topics below). Then each of you talks for two minutes about your memory—as the others *really* listen.

SAMPLE TOPICS: Bathtime when you were very young—before you went to school. What was the tub like, where was the soap, what toys did you play with, what did the washcloth feel like, who bathed you? Be that little tot in that water.

Your "cookie person." When you were very young, you probably knew someone who acted as your "cookie person"—a man or woman outside your family who really cared for you. This person may have actually baked cookies for you, may have driven you to the library to open the world of books to you, may have told you stories about the old country, may have done a thousand other things to let you know how welcome you were in his or her company. Who was your cookie person and what did she or he do?

When we talk about our cookie persons we ought to remind ourselves how important we were to them. Our parents probably warned us not to be pests and not to "wear out our welcomes." In truth, we most likely gave a lift to our cookie person's day.

A good follow-up to this discussion is for everyone to think of someone we might be a cookie person to, someone who would really welcome our interest in them.

Early sex games. You might have played "doctor" with your cousins when you were very small. You might not have played "Spin the Bottle" till you were in your teens. Either way, your early explorations with the opposite sex were probably a significant chapter in your life and a good reflection of the values you had already picked up about relationships between the sexes, sexuality, and your feelings about yourself.

The first time you remember being treated differently because of your sex, color, religion, or any other characteristic you want to explore. The starter asks everyone to think about the particular characteristic. A girl might remember the scratchy starched dress she had to wear to church; a boy might remember being told, "You're the man of the family now"; a Black child, a Jewish child, an immigrant child—all would have their special, possibly painful, possibly strange, possibly joyous memories.

A homecoming. When you were very young, and one or both of your parents came home after having been away, either for the day or for a longer time, how did they greet you? How did you greet them? How did you feel about seeing them?

Your very earliest memory. What is it about? About how old were you? What were your surroundings like?

Other topics: roller skates, bikes, canoes, test papers, singing, art work, books you loved, parties, junior prom, first sweetheart, and so forth.

We learn so much about each other by discovering the experiences in our lives that have made the deepest impressions. We also learn about ourselves, since attitudes that we didn't even know we had still come through to impress themselves indelibly upon our memories.

8

GETTING TO KNOW ME

The Greek philosopher Diogenes was washing lentils when he was visited by his friend Aristippus, a great favorite of the king. Upon seeing Diogenes engaged in such a humble task, Aristippus exclaimed, "If you had only learned to flatter King Denys, you would not have to be washing lentils!" "And you," retorted Diogenes, "if you had only learned to live on lentils, would not have to flatter King Denys."

Both these ancients knew what they wanted out of life. Do you? Too many of us have never been encouraged to think about what the good life is for us. We don't know ourselves. We don't know what's important to us. We don't know what our abilities are. We don't know what we want out of life. The following conversations with 10-year-old Hilary are typical.

HILARY'S BEST FRIEND: "What do you want to do today?"

HILARY: "I don't care."

HILARY'S GRANDFATHER: "What's your favorite subject in school?"

HILARY: "I don't like any of 'em."

HILARY'S TEACHER: "What do you like to do on weekends?"

HILARY: "I dunno."

Poor Hilary. She has never been encouraged to think about the many possibilities life has to offer—and about her role in choosing which fruits to pluck from it. Too many children are like Hilary. They don't know what's important to them. They don't know what their abilities are. They don't know what they want out of life. They don't know themselves.

We need to discover what we value. We need to analyze our lives, to see whether what we do goes along with what we say. Are we living our lives according to the values we say we hold? If not, are our values wrong—or do we want to change the patterns of our days?

Too many of us go along from day to day doing things a certain way because we've always done them that way—because that's the way our parents did them before us, or for some other unexamined reason. Most of us use no more than fifteen percent of our capability. We rarely have any idea where our full powers could lead us. By making an extra effort to examine ourselves and our lives, we can unleash more of our precious powers.

LEARNING TO EVALUATE OURSELVES

One of Joey's favorite kindergarten activities was "Connect-the-dots." One day, he brought home a paper marked "minus 1." His mother commended him on his good work, but as she was looking at it, she found another mistake. When she pointed it out to Joey so that he could correct it, he said, "No, there can't be another mistake. Because—see here—Miss Brown wrote 'minus one' on the paper. That means there's only *one* mistake."

His mother gently showed Joey the place where his line had gone first to 25, then to 24. "Doesn't twenty-four come before twenty-five?" she asked. "Yes," said Joey. "Then shouldn't the line have gone from twenty-three to twenty-four—and then to twenty-five?" she asked. "Yes," said Joey. "Then that's a mistake you can fix," said his mother. "No, it can't be," Joey insisted. "If that was a mistake, Miss Brown would have put 'minus two.' "

No amount of persuasion on his mother's part that teachers can make mistakes, too, could shake Joey's conviction that his paper had only one mistake. Already—at the age of 5—Joey considered an external symbol, a reflection of someone else's evaluation of his work, more important than the truth.

One 45-year-old lawyer said that she yearns for the old days when she knew just how she was doing because of the marks on her report card. "Now I have to judge myself," she complained. "And that's so hard to do—it's easier just to let somebody else give me a grade." But we have to learn to measure ourselves, since we are the ultimate arbiters of our own lives.

Ruth Moulton, M.D., a New York psychoanalyst, compares the person who depends on other people's evaluations to the cold-blooded animal who has to depend on the outside temperature: "Since frogs can't make their own body warmth, they dig in the mud and hibernate when the snow and ice come. Insecure personalities are like this, too. When they hear a kind word, they're nice and warm. But harsh words will freeze their very marrow. And when they don't know which words to believe, they don't know whether to stay underground or to come out into the sunlight."

When you can accurately appraise what you're good at and what you're not so good at, then you won't be overly affected by the judgments of others. It is important to recognize that leading our lives to please others and basing our feelings about ourselves on what other people think is like trying to get an accurate picture of ourselves by looking in a mirror in the dark.

Your children will be making countless decisions about their lives in the years to come. To help them make the right ones, you can help them to know themselves. Only then can they be true to themselves and do the best for themselves—and ultimately, for others, too.

Some strategies that are especially helpful for self-knowledge are included in the next chapter.

9

STRATEGIES FOR GETTING TO KNOW YOURSELF

The strategies grouped together here all focus somewhat differently on self-knowledge. Try them in any order you like and you are bound to end up knowing yourselves a little bit better.

15. Personal Coat of Arms
16. Are You Someone Who . . . ?
17. Spending
18. The Here and Now Wheel
19. Celebrity Room
20. Archeological Find: Your Room
21. If I Were a Book
22. Moments to Remember
23. I Am . . .
24. No Red Carnation
25. Alligator River
26. Brown Bag
27. This Is the Week That Was
28. Contract with Yourself
29. Obituary
30. We Are What We Wear

Strategy 15

PERSONAL COAT OF ARMS

How would you like to have your own personal Coat of Arms? An impressive heraldic emblem that would symbolize what's important in your life? You don't have to be of royal lineage to have this. All you have to do is *think* about what really matters to you.

TIME: Any time the family is together. Fun to do with guests of any age.

PLACE: Kitchen table, dinner table, anywhere you can write.

EQUIPMENT: Large sheets of paper and pencils.

PROCEDURE: Everyone draws an outline of a coat of arms like the one on page 82, and divides it into six sections, numbering them as shown. Each person answers the first five questions below by drawing pictures, designs, or symbols in the appropriate sections. The drawings don't have to be good as artwork, and they don't have to make sense to anyone but the person who made them. The sixth question is the only one to be answered in words.

THE QUESTIONS:

1. What is your greatest personal achievement so far?
2. What are three things you are good at?
3. What is one thing that other people can do to make you happy?
4. What is one thing you are striving to attain?
5. What would you do if you had one year to live and were guaranteed success in whatever you attempted?
6. What three things would you most like to have said about you if you died today?

Then everyone examines his or her Coat of Arms and writes an "Ah-hah!" statement (see page 49) about it. People then

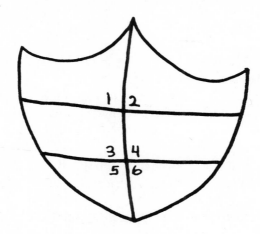

share their drawings, explaining them to each other. Everyone has the option of keeping his or her drawings private. Some may want to post theirs on the Family Bulletin Board (see page 150). VARIATIONS: You may substitute different questions for any of the six above, such as:

- What makes you happy?
- What makes you sad?
- What are you afraid of?
- What is something about which you would never budge?
- What material possession is most important to you?
- What is your greatest failure?
- What is a personal motto that you live by?

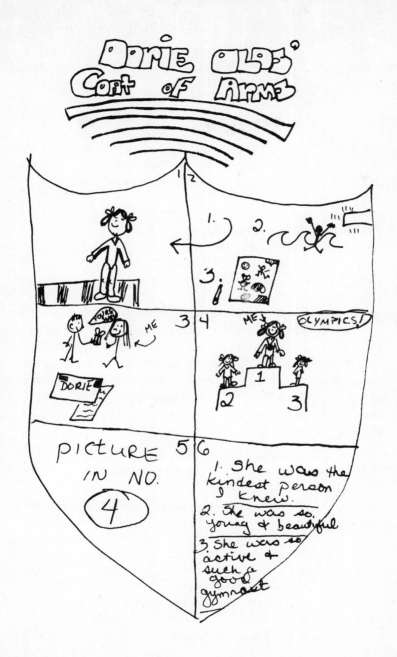

Strategy 16

ARE YOU SOMEONE WHO . . .?

No thrill of discovery is greater than those that come from self-exploration. This strategy helps us find out more about ourselves, and also more about those who are close to us.

TIME: Any time.
PLACE: Anywhere you can write.
EQUIPMENT: Paper and pencils.
PROCEDURE: Draw lines on your paper setting up a column for each person in your family including yourself. Number down the left-side margin from 1 to 20.

The starter reads aloud twenty questions and their key words —either from the list below or some you make up yourself. By each number, write down the key word for each question. Then answer for yourselves, and also for the way you see the other members of your family, by writing down, Yes, No, Sometimes, or I Don't Know in the appropriate columns.

SAMPLE QUESTIONS:
Are you someone who . . .

1. likes to be first in line? (Key Word: (first)
2. would take part in a protest demonstration? (demontration)
3. would want to be a migrant farmworker for a summer? (migrant)
4. uses swear words in public? (swear)
5. would never smoke pot with your children? (pot)
6. likes to go swimming in the nude? (nude)
7. likes to write letters? (write)
8. likes to receive letters? (receive)
9. has never thought about killing yourself? (suicide)
10. wants to be famous? (fame)
11. writes letters to your representatives in Congress? (Congress)

12. would like to learn to meditate? (meditate)
13. likes to go to the beach in winter? (beach)
14. throws candy wrappers on the sidewalk? (sidewalk)
15. likes to be with people? (people)
16. watches TV every day? (TV)
17. never wants to get married? (single)
18. says what you think even when it gets you in trouble? (trouble)
19. can receive a compliment easily? (receive)
20. gives compliments often? (give)
21. likes to play with babies? (babies)
22. makes a special point of watching the sun set? (sunset)
23. finds it easy to apologize? (apologize)
24. likes to work hard? (work)
25. is shy around people you don't know? (shy)

After answering all the questions, you each write an "Ah-hah!" statement (see page 49) about what you learned about yourself.

You all share what you put down for each other, as well as for yourselves. It can be a revelation to "see ourselves as others see us," but it can also be disturbing. So this discussion needs to be handled with tact and sensitivity to everyone's feelings.

After doing this strategy, you're likely to know yourself better. You're also more likely to think about the messages you send to the members of your family, how well you know each other, and how open you are willing to be with each other.

Strategy 17

SPENDING

All of us have only a limited amount of time, and most of us have a limited amount of money. How we choose to spend our time and money gives a clue to what we value. Or does it? Sometimes we fill our days and empty our pockets without much thought. Only upon later reflection do we decide that we might have done things differently.

Children don't value time, which seems to stretch on endlessly before them, but they usually do care about money, which they have much less of. This strategy helps them to appreciate time and money, and the connections between what they say they value and what they really do.

TIME: Any time.

PLACE: Any place you can write.

EQUIPMENT: Paper and pencils, kitchen timer.

PROCEDURE: Everyone writes down responses to one of the categories below. After you have written them, look for a pattern in your answers. Ask yourself whether you like what you see. Then each of you gets two minutes to share your feelings about your pattern: why you like it or don't like it, and if you don't like it—what else you could do.

CATEGORIES:

How I spent . . .

- the last five or six Saturday afternoons
- the last five or six weekends
- the last five or six Sundays
- the last two special long weekends
- every evening last week
- my last two birthdays
- my last ten dollars (change amount as appropriate for younger children and adults)
- my last ten dollars of discretionary income (money that didn't have to go for essentials like lunches, bus fare, and other basic, necessary items)

FOLLOW-UPS:

- "Ah-hah!" (Strategy 2, page 49)
- Save all your papers, do the strategy again in three months, and see what changes have taken place.

This strategy helps people to see patterns in their habits of spending time and money. Once they see a pattern, they can decide whether or not they like it—and how it can be changed.

Strategy 18

THE HERE AND NOW WHEEL

From the expressions on people's faces as they sat down to dinner, it had obviously been a bad day for some members of the Hatcher family. The air was heavy with tension as brothers and parents alternated between sniping at each other and retreating into sullen silence. But no one really talked about his or her feelings, until Mother suggested doing "The Here and Now Wheel."

When Father's turn came to identify his feelings of the moment, he began with "tired" and ended with "annoyed." He went on to explain that he was annoyed because a chore he had asked the boys to do four days ago was still undone. "You're always quick enough to ask me to drive you here or give you money for that—but when I ask you to do something and you don't do it, that makes me feel as if whatever I ask you to do is unimportant—and I don't matter much to you, either."

"Well, why didn't you tell us how you felt before this?" asked Dan, 13. "We didn't know it was so important to you."

"Okay," Father answered. "I'm telling you now."

The Here and Now Wheel can help people to get in touch with their own feelings—and to verbalize them at the moment.

Our feelings are often elusive. Unless we make deliberate efforts to track them down, it is sometimes hard to know exactly how we do feel about things. The Here and Now Wheel helps us zero in on our feelings in a specific situation, with specific people, during specific experiences.

TIME: Any time, but especially meaningful at a time when emotions are running high: during an argument, when a decision has to be made, or after an upsetting experience.

PLACE: Anywhere you can write.

EQUIPMENT: Paper and pencils.

PROCEDURE: Everyone draws a circle and divides it in four sections (see illustration below). In each quarter, write a word or phrase, or draw a picture, describing your feelings at this very moment (e.g., "confused," "ashamed," "mischievous," "happy"). Write a sentence about one of the feelings you expressed. Below the circle, put the date and the time of day.

Break up into groups of two or three to talk about the feelings you wrote down. This approach should help you reveal your true feelings to each other and, as a result, be better able to deal with them.

Doing several Here and Now Wheels on different days illustrates the ways that feelings change.

Today you may not even remember something that once consumed you with its importance. Today you may go into gales of laughter over something that once sent you into paroxysms of shame. The very act of identifying and acknowledging our feelings often allows us to deal with them and the problems that engendered them in a positive way.

VARIATION: Unwritten Wheel: Around the breakfast table, before eating dinner, in the car, or anywhere else, someone can ask everyone to name three or four feelings you have right at that moment. You may choose to talk about the feelings or not. Just expressing them helps you to know yourselves and each other a little bit better.

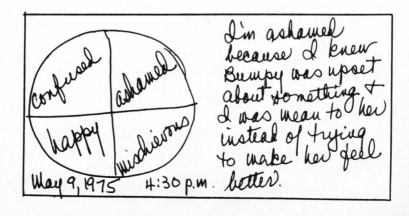

Strategy 19

CELEBRITY ROOM

In New York City, Bloomingdale's department store features a constantly changing display of model rooms, which show elegant decorator furniture and accessories. The store's decorating staff regularly interviews celebrities, and then designs rooms to fit their personalities. In this strategy, each of you designs your own model room.

TIME: Any time.
PLACE: Anywhere.
EQUIPMENT: Kitchen timer.
PROCEDURE: Imagine you are being interviewed about your ideal room. It can be a bedroom, workshop, study, playroom, living room, any room. Each person gets two minutes to describe his or her ideal room. Others may ask one question apiece of the focus person. ("What colors would you have in it?" "Would you have music?" "What would you have on the walls?")

After you have all described your ideal rooms, each of you thinks out loud about what you could do to make your present room closer to your ideal.

Strategy 20

ARCHEOLOGICAL FIND: YOUR ROOM

Archeologists have learned many things about people of former times by analyzing the remains of the places where these people once lived. What could an archeologist learn about *you* from analyzing your room?

TIME: Any time.
PLACE: Anywhere.
EQUIPMENT: Kitchen timer.

PROCEDURE: Imagine this situation: It is 2,000 years from now. Iwanna Pheindit, an archeologist interested in twentieth-century Americans, has stumbled across an important find: your room, perfectly preserved just as it is now. Each of you gets three minutes to tell everything that an archeologist could discover about your values and your daily life from a careful examination of the items in your room right this minute.

FOLLOW-UPS: A discussion centered around the ways people might like to change their rooms to reflect different things about themselves.

A work project in which everyone makes some changes.

Strategy 21

IF I WERE A BOOK

Every book is different from every other book—just as every person's life, values, and personality are different from those of everyone else. The book that you would write—or the one you'd be the leading character in—would be different from mine.

TIME: Any time.

PLACE: Anywhere.

EQUIPMENT: Kitchen timer, paper and crayons to design book jackets (optional).

PROCEDURE: Each gets three minutes to answer, "If I were a book, what would I be like?" People can categorize themselves as books of adventure, mystery, romance, psychological exploration, history, science, or how-to. (We know one youngster who sees herself as a joke book.) You can then think in terms of size, weight, table of contents, jacket cover, dedication, illustrations, and so forth.

VARIATIONS: This same approach could be used to imagine your-selves as:

· a movie
· a television series
· a magazine
· a record

FOLLOW-UP: Design book jackets; ads for movie or TV series; magazine or album covers.

Strategy 22

MOMENTS TO REMEMBER

Few of us will write our memoirs. Most of us will never immortalize on paper the many special moments in our lives. But we can all enrich our lives by seeking out and preserving these treasures for ourselves.

TIME: Any time.
PLACE: Anywhere you can write.
EQUIPMENT: Notebooks or paper, pencils, kitchen timer.
PROCEDURE: The starter asks everyone to think of a special moment in his or her life, designating one particular kind of moment like those in the list below. Ten minutes are given to write about it. Fill in as many details as possible to capture the moment. After everyone has finished writing, share your moments with each other—always remembering that anyone who does not want to talk has the option of keeping his or her moment private.
SPECIAL MOMENTS:

· My happiest moment
· My most embarrassing experience
· My earliest memory

- My saddest moment
- My angriest moment
- My most frightening experience
- My most loving moment
- My most disappointing moment
- My proudest moment
- My most carefree moment
- My favorite dream

Strategy 23

I AM . . .

The way we think about ourselves dictates the things we do and the way we relate to other people—in essence, the way we live our lives. This strategy encourages people of all ages to think about themselves in new ways.

TIME: Any time.

PLACE: Anywhere you can write.

EQUIPMENT: Pencils and ten small pieces of paper for each person.

PROCEDURE: Write down "I am" on each slip of paper and then finish the sentences, ending up with ten statements. Put the ten slips of paper in order, according to the personal importance of each statement. Take turns reading out loud the three statements each considers most important.

In the discussion that follows about these pictures of yourself as you see yourself, these questions might be tossed out:

- Do you see yourself as what you *do* or what you *are?*
- Do you see yourself in your roles (student, son, husband, mother, etc.)?
- Do you define yourself by your physical characteristics?

- Do you identify yourself by your personality traits?
- Do you define yourself by the way others see you?
- Are there conflicts between your inner and outer self?
- Examine your priorities: Where do you surprise people?
- Listening to other people, are there things you didn't think of before that you'd like to put down now?

VARIATIONS: Put a check by those characteristics you would like to improve in some way. Rank the checked slips in order of importance, and discuss ways you might make improvements, and ways other people could help you.

Rank the slips in order according to how much you would like to see your own children make these statements. If there are some you would definitely not want them to make, think about why you made them and whether you want to change in some way.

Strategy 24

NO RED CARNATION

How do we see ourselves? What sorts of things stand out about us, to us? While beauty may be only "skin-deep," people's concepts of what they look like can affect their total self-concept, especially in youth. This strategy helps us to see and share our images of ourselves.

TIME: Any time.
PLACE: Anywhere.
EQUIPMENT: Full-length mirror (optional).
PROCEDURE: Imagine that you are setting up an appointment by telephone with someone you have never met. You will be meeting in a crowded place, and you are asked "How will I know

you?" You're not allowed to say, "I'll be wearing a red carnation." You have to provide a description of yourself.

If you have a full-length mirror handy, everyone looks in it for thirty seconds. Then you go around the group, each giving the description of yourself that you would give to a total stranger.

After each of you has spoken, the other family members add validating statements about the person that would help them be recognized.

Then people think about these two questions:

· What kinds of things can people who have known you for a year see in you that are not apparent on the surface?
· In the next year, what would you want to develop within you to make you more recognizably beautiful?

Strategy 25

ALLIGATOR RIVER

"Cecil was rotten and selfish, the way he treated Alice," said a 15-year-old boy, talking with a group of teenagers.

"Alice should have known how Cecil would react," responded an older girl.

"Yeah, but she was trying to be honest," another girl said.

"It's her mother I blame. She should have talked to Alice."

"But she was giving Alice a chance to make her own mind up."

"Yeah, but she could have at least sat down and talked about what might have happened . . ."

"Cecil had no compassion, but what about some compassion for him? You have to take into account that he was really upset."

The Cecil and Alice these young people are talking about are leading characters in a fable that poses questions of virginity, fidelity, honesty, exploitation, parental resonsibility, violence, and love, and gets people thinking about these values in a new and very specific way.

TIME: Any time teenagers and adults are together. (Younger children are not close enough to some of these issues to give or get as much from this strategy.)

PLACE: Anywhere.

EQUIPMENT: None.

PROCEDURE: The starter tells this story:

"Alice and Cecil are sweethearts who live on opposite shores of an alligator-infested river. One day a storm washes away the bridge over Alligator River. Alice asks Sinbad, a sailor, to take her across in his boat, and he agrees—on one condition: that Alice sleep with him. Confused and uncertain, Alice asks her mother what she should do, but her mother says, 'You're old enough to make your own decision. I don't think I should get involved.' Alice accepts Sinbad's terms and sleeps with him. He then ferries her across the river, where she meets Cecil. Overjoyed to be with her lover, she tells him what she had to do to see him. He becomes furious, calls her names, and sends her away. As she runs through the woods, Alice meets Edward. She tells him her story, and he goes after Cecil and beats him up. Watching the beating, Alice laughs heartily."

After hearing the story, everyone ranks the five characters, according to his or her own value system, from most to least offensive. After everyone has made up his or her own list, family members talk about the relative rankings, and why they ranked the characters as they did.

Some questions that might be tossed into the discussion:

· How do you think you would react if you were Alice/Cecil?
· What could various people in this story have done differently to give it a happier ending?
· What could people in the story have done that would have made things worse?
· Why do you think the characters behaved as they did?

Strategy 26

BROWN BAG

Most young children love to cut out pictures from magazines. This strategy is especially suitable for children from 4 to 8, who can be helped to turn this activity into a thought-provoking search for values.

TIME: Any time. Rainy days, weekends, or vacation days are ideal.
PLACE: A room where you can spread out and make a mess.
EQUIPMENT: Old magazines, scissors, paste, large grocery bags.
PROCEDURE: Each participant decorates a bag with pictures and words depicting people, ideas, or activities she or he values. Inside the bag go clippings, pictures, and words that she or he is confused about.

Eight-year-old Gina, for example, pasted on the outside of her bag pictures representing physical fitness, animals, and babies. Inside she put some pictures representing various occupations she thought she might want to follow some day, a poem she liked but did understand, and a photo of children of different races.

After everyone's bag is completed, each collage-maker discusses the outside and as much of the inside contents as she or he wants.

Strategy 27

THIS IS THE WEEK THAT WAS

Our lives tend to go by in a blur of experiences, feelings and actions. We often fail to recognize which ones are most important. Only by sitting back and consciously examining the patterns of our days can we put our lives in perspective. This strategy helps us do this on a weekly basis.

TIME: During the weekend, when we can reflect about the preceding week.

PLACE: Anywhere.

EQUIPMENT: None (personal diaries, paper and pencils optional).

PROCEDURE: The starter tosses out one or more of the following questions. People may answer them out loud, reflect in private about them, or record their answers in a personal diary.

SAMPLE QUESTIONS:

· What was the high point of my week?
· What was the low point?
· Was I in complete agreement with anyone about anything this week?
· Was I in strong disagreement?
· Did I make any changes in my life this week?
· What plans did I make? (buying tickets, planning to meet someone, etc.)
· What did I put off that I should have done?
· What were three choices that I made?
· What risks did I take?
· How can I make next week better than this week?
· Did I do anything to help anyone else? What—and how did I feel about it (happy, resentful, etc.)? Did I feel appreciated or taken for granted?
· Did I ask for help? How did I feel about that? Did I get the help I needed? If not, how can I get it?
· Did I make someone I care for feel good about him/herself?
· Did anyone make me feel good about myself?

Strategy 28

CONTRACT WITH YOURSELF

In line with the sixth and seventh steps in the process of valuing, a value cannot exist without action. This strategy encourages you to act in a very specific way. It can follow any discussion, any other strategy, or any thinking about a particular issue in your life. It forces you to make a commitment to yourself, to promise yourself in writing that you will do something to make your life better.

TIME: Any time.
PLACE: Anywhere you can write.
EQUIPMENT: Paper and pen.
PROCEDURE: Write out a contract, following the form of the one on page 99. Limit your intended action to one, or a series of *specific* actions, rather than a large, long-range goal. Instead of saying, for example, "I promise myself that I will lose twenty pounds," be specific about what you are actually going to do to lose the weight: "I am going to eat no more than 1,000 calories every day." Don't say, "I'll work harder on my music," but say instead, "I'll practice playing the guitar for seven hours every week."

The contract has a space for the signature of a close friend who acts as your witness and who indicates his or her commitment to remind you of your contract provisions on whatever date you agree upon. Involving another person adds an extra incentive to you to carry through on your plans. It also allows you to share your goal with someone you trust and lets that person assume a very special role in your life. The two of you plan to celebrate together the completion of your contract.

When you fulfill the terms of your contract, you will really have something to celebrate, some way in which you took action to improve your life. At this point, you may want to draw up a new contract toward the same goal, or toward another one. You will probably find that you like doing business with yourself!

THE CONTRACT:

I, _____, in order to _____
　　　　　　　　　(your name)

_____,
(goal)

promise myself that I will _____.
　　　　　　　　　　　　　　　(action you promise to take)

This contract will be fulfilled on _____.
　　　　　　　　　　　　　　　　　　(date)

Witnessed by _____, who promises to
　　　　　　　　　(signature of friend)

contact me on _____, so that we can celebrate
　　　　　　　(date, before due date)

the completion of this contract on _____.
　　　　　　　　　　　　　　　　　　(date, after due date)

_____
(date)

　　　　　　　　　　　　　_____
　　　　　　　　　　　　　　　(your signature)

Strategy 29

OBITUARY

When the notice of the death of a prominent person appears on the obituary page of a major newspaper, it serves as a summing-up of that person's life. It always indicates the reasons for the person's prominence. And it often gives important milestones in their life, the flavor of their personality, and some of the person's previously quoted statements about the significant aspects of their life.

By focusing on such a summing-up, this strategy encourages us to look at our lives in a new way. It makes us think about the way we would like to be remembered. And it makes us question whether we are living our lives in accordance with our values.

TIME: Any, except during periods of death-related stress. (See Note to Parents, page 101.)

PLACE: Anywhere you can write.

EQUIPMENT: Paper and pencils.

PROCEDURE: The starter either hands out copies of the following questionnaire or reads out the parts of sentences, for people to copy and complete. Each of you fills out your own obituary notice. Then you each write an "Ah-hah!" statement (page 49) about what you have learned about yourself and your life from this strategy. Finally, you each write a statement beginning, "I resolve . . ." to make your life better in some way.

Share your obituaries, your "Ah-hah!" statements, and your resolutions with each other (always with the option of passing for anyone who wants to).

THE OBITUARY:

_____, age ___, died yesterday.
(*your name*)

At the time of his/her death, s/he was working on _____

_____.

S/he will be remembered especially for _____.

S/he wanted to be remembered for _____.

S/he felt that his/her most significant contribution to the world

was _____.

S/he will be missed most sorely by _____.

His/her greatest desire was to _____.

His/her last wish was _____.

According to his/her wishes, the body will be _____.

_____ led the memorial service, which took
(*person you would want*)

place at _____.

Survivors are _____.

Those who wish to commemorate _____'s life may
(*your name*)

_____.

(*send flowers, contribute to a favorite charity, do something else*)

VARIATION: Everyone draws a line down the center of a sheet of paper. On the left, write the obituary as it would appear if you were to die today. On the right, as you would like it to appear if you died twenty years from now. Discuss what you might start doing now to make the obituary that will eventually appear reflect what you want your life to stand for.

Note to Parents: Thoughts of death generate anxiety in most of us, adults and children alike. In leading this strategy, it is important to be sensitive to your family's feelings. It is best not to introduce this strategy immediately after a death in the family or when anxiety levels about death are especially high among any family members. The strategy works best when you keep the emphasis positive, stressing what we can learn from it about living, rather than stressing our mortality.

Strategy 30

WE ARE WHAT WE WEAR

"You can't wear those dirty, torn jeans to Grandma's house." "It's crazy to wear those high heels to school—you can't even walk in them, let alone run the way you usually do." "Uh-uh— no see-through blouses for any daughter of mine!"

The clothes closet is one of the most trod-upon battlegrounds between parents and children, largely because both generations realize that whenever we get dressed, we make statements about ourselves. A recent study of 400 college students found that their personalities and the way they dressed were closely related, and that analyzing their personality traits enabled strangers to predict how the students would dress. We all tend to get impressions of people by the way they dress, and, of course, others get impressions of us, as well.

TIME: Any time people are dressed in the clothes they normally wear to school or work.

PLACE: Anywhere you can write.

EQUIPMENT: Pencils and paper.

PROCEDURE: Everyone divides a sheet of paper into two columns. In the first, you list every item of clothing and jewelry you are wearing that day, and in the second you write down what you want your clothing to say about you. For example, next to "platform shoes," you might say, "up with the latest styles"; "old jeans"—"I don't want people to think I'm trying to look rich"; "team jackets"—"I want everyone to know I'm on the gym team."

After you have finished with your lists, you might talk about these questions:

· Are there certain times when you want to convey a different impression?
· Do you dress differently for church, for school, and for parties? Why or why not?
· Would you dress differently for a job interview than for a rock concert? Why or why not?
· How would/do you feel about wearing a uniform to school?
· Suppose you were offered someone's entire wardrobe for free? Whose would you want? Whose wouldn't you accept?

10

I AM LOVABLE AND CAPABLE

Greg, 8, helps himself to mashed potatoes as he sighs, "Boy, was Miss Barton mean to me today!"

His father turns and says, "What did you do *this* time? And don't be such a pig with those potatoes. The rest of us have to eat, too, you know. Watch out—your milk!"

"Uh-oh!" exclaims Greg, mesmerized by the sight of the spreading puddle of milk beginning to seep down the side of the table. "I'm sorry—I'll wipe it up."

"Never mind," says his mother, rushing in with a sponge. "You'll just make a bigger mess. When will you stop being so clumsy?"

By the time Greg's spilled milk was cleaned up, he had lost his appetite for dinner. But this was one night that his "vulture" feasted heavily.

Practically every one of us has a vulture like Greg's. One of its huge claws is plunged deeply and tenaciously into the very core of our being, while the other ravenously tears open the surrounding flesh, leaving us bleeding and in pain. Its sharp beak is constantly attacking us, constantly feeding on us. And most of us feed our vulture very well.

Every time we tell ourselves that we're not good enough and every time we deprecate ourselves to others, our vulture stabs its beak into the places where we are the most vulnerable. Other people feed our vulture, too. Every time someone else makes us feel inadequate, our vulture takes another mouthful. The vulture builds up its strength by weakening ours. We feed the vultures of other people—even those we love the most. Whenever we criticize, needle, and call names, we give someone's vulture a tasty morsel.

But we *can* starve and weaken our vultures till they leave us free of their painful hold. Free to recognize ourselves as lovable, capable human beings, who are worthy of love and respect.

Our vultures get in the way of our search for values. We need to prize what we value. But we can't do that unless we prize ourselves. We have to feel good enough about ourselves to learn our wants and needs, accept them as legitimate, and feel worthy of asking for what we want. So many of us have so little self-esteem that we don't feel we deserve much out of life. We take what we can get, grateful for a slim portion of the good life, instead of trying to get our fair share.

GROWING UP IN A RED-PENCIL MENTALITY

Most of us have grown up in a climate of correction. Our mistakes and our shortcomings have been underlined, while our strengths and our accomplishments have been taken for granted or overlooked. We have been trained to be humble and modest. Far too many of us have ended up thinking that we're not anything much and that our lives are not very precious.

Some parents feel that focusing on their children's good points will give them a "swelled head" and make it hard for them to get along with other people. Yet studies show that children with a healthy sense of self-esteem give much more to life and get much more out of it. They set higher goals for themselves and are more likely to achieve their objectives. They are more popular than children who don't think much of themselves. They are more likely to go after what they want—and to get it.

"That's all very well," you may say. "But kids have to live in the real world, too. If we keep telling them at home how great they are, they'll be expecting that wherever they go. And when they don't get that kind of treatment, they'll be sunk."

But if we make sure that our children appreciate themselves, they will be better able to withstand the "slings and arrows" they receive in the outside world. We can explain that not all people are as validating as we are at home. Even if vultures thrive in the outside world, we can make them shrivel up at home.

Most of us can probably summon up countless episodes when we have been hurt by parents, teachers, and others close to us. Now by remembering our own feelings, we can be more caring and aware of our children.

We can create a climate of validation in our homes. Instead of a red-pencil mentality, we can develop a blue-ribbon mentality. We can focus on the positive aspects of our lives—the things we do well, the times we feel good about ourselves.

THE COMPLIMENT-FLICK

Most of us have been red-penciled so often in the past that we don't know how to accept a word of praise. We have developed the "compliment-flick" reflex. When someone tells us, "You look lovely in that dress," we say as quickly as possible, "And I just love your necklace." We flick off the compliment just as fast as we can. A recent study found that eight out of ten people praised feel obligated to return the kind word as soon as possible. This reflex is common. But it is not healthy.

We should be able to enjoy a sincere compliment, to let it flow through our bodies and warm us to the core. Most of us have to be retrained to learn how to do this. We can compare ourselves to a middle-aged man who has lived on a diet of soda pop, candy bars, and potato chips all his life. When he begins to receive good nutrition, he goes through a transitional period when the vegetables and fruits and fresh fish are hard to swallow. He has to learn to enjoy and taste and savor the better nutrition. Once he does, he won't go back to his old diet. Once we and our children learn how to accept compliments, we won't go back to the old red-pencil mentality that makes us flick them off as fast as we can.

VALIDATION TRAINING IN THE FAMILY

In the Values Clarification workshops given regularly by the senior author, he speaks to elementary, junior high, and high school students from all over the country. He asks these young people, "From whom would you like more validation?" Over and over again, they say, "My mother." Or "my father." Then they rush to say, "I get *some,* of course. But I want more." We *all* want more. No one among us—child or adult—is walking around suffering from over-validation. We all *need* more. We all can learn to *give* more.

The concept of validation embraces an appreciation of ourselves. Few of us see the beautiful things about ourselves—or publicly recognize the wonderful things about those we love. We need a climate of validation in our homes, and we can train ourselves to produce it.

Those of us who rear children tend to forget about validating them in the face of our obligation to socialize them. We find ourselves saying, "Don't," "Hurry up," "Quit that," "Stand up straight," "Get your elbows off the table," "Chew with your mouth closed," "Wash the dirt off your neck," "Brush your teeth," "Turn off the TV and do your homework."

We can't get rid of all of this. Nor should we. We have to teach our children what they need to know to live in society. But we need to watch the balance in our homes. Are we constantly correcting, ordering, and scolding? Do we neglect to tell our children all the ways in which they are lovable and capable? If so, we are feeding vultures, not nourishing egos.

We must remember to say the good things, too. We have to tell our children, "When you come home, you fill the whole house with sunshine." We have to let them know, "I really have a good time when you and I go out together." We have to tell them in many ways that they are lovable and capable.

We all need more chances to focus on what we've done well and what we feel good about. Most of us are only too aware of the areas where we fall short. We need people to tell us where we are strong.

We have to encourage our children to make efforts to validate each other. Too often, the accepted form of banter among children is a constant barrage of insults. Flurries of "killer statements" characterize many exchanges among brothers and sisters. But children in the same family *can* learn how to appreciate each other and to show it.

How can we train ourselves to give and receive validation? First, a family can develop a store of stock phrases like the examples below. They can be hilarious in context and can create a lot of family fun. On one day, the family can agree that every time anyone is complimented, she or he must answer, "I wholeheartedly agree with you." Family members will praise each other, just to hear this. On another day, everyone has to respond with, "How perceptive of you to notice." A few other such phrases are:

· I always knew you had good judgment/taste/insight.
· I *am* wonderful, aren't I?
· I really am a beautiful person.
· You are so lucky to be related to me.

How we all gulp and grimace and grin and shrug as we force ourselves to make these bold self-validating statements! The laughter that greets the stock phrases helps to dispel some of our awkwardness and lets us acknowledge validation.

The family can then go on to more formal and more poignant validating sessions. After dinner once a week, you all might stand and make a circle with your arms around each other. In this close setting, validations are especially meaningful. They won't have to be laughed off with any stock phrases, but can be easily accepted and savored.

Here are some other ways your family can validate each other:

Before Thanksgiving dessert is served, you might do a round of the people you are thankful for. In one family, a 7-year-old Brownie was "thankful for my sister who delivered my Girl Scout cookies when I had the flu." Calvin, 17, was "thankful that Grandpa had such a will to live and went for therapy after his stroke." Calvin's father was "thankful that I have a loving and responsible brother who carried the load for all the out-of-town family members like me when our Dad was stricken." And a young mother looked adoringly at her husband as she spoke her gratitude to him, "because I know how much courage it took for him to agree to adopt our little brown babies—and because we are so happy now."

Every now and then, everyone sits down to write out three validations for one family member—and then hides them somewhere in the receiver's room. The receiver then brings the validation notes down to the next meal and reads them out loud. Notes keep popping up over a period of days—or even weeks or months—but the validations are always fresh and new.

SETTING AN ATMOSPHERE OF COMFORT AND CARING

Robert Frost described home as "the place where, when you have to go there . . . they have to let you in." Home can be so much more than this! It can be a refuge from the world, a place where you know people really care about you, where they help you nurse your wounds and give you strength and sustenance to go out to meet life's challenges.

No home is ever completely like this. We all have our own needs, which may conflict with those of other family members. We have our passions and our angers. But we can aim toward an atmosphere of comfort and caring.

In our Values Clarification workshops, we always try to set such an atmosphere in the first few minutes that we come together. We welcome everyone. We inquire about everyone's problems. Since many people come long distances, we make every effort to see that creature needs are taken care of, that people have a bed, a place to eat, and whatever rides they need. Sometimes we have to call upon the other participants. They never fail to give this help. This is comfort and caring.

This same kind of atmosphere can be in the home. When one person has a problem, the rest of us can help. We help ungrudgingly, knowing our turn will come. For example, Barney had planned to ride his bike to school. Just as he was about to take off, he discovered a flat tire. If he walks, he'll be late to class. He has no time to fix the flat. He brings his problem to the family, and is cheered when his brother, Carl, offers to lend him his bike—and also offers to fix the flat for him, since he knows that Barney has a busy day ahead of him. This is comfort and caring.

When someone drops something or spills something or breaks something in the Simon household, someone else comes running to clean it up. This is comfort and caring.

Eileen has been saving up for a special backpack, when she sees a newspaper ad announcing a one-day sale. Since she cannot get to the store that day, she brings her problem to the family. Her father, who has the most flexible schedule on that day, offers to go. This is comfort and caring.

All these incidents have taken place in families where people have learned to ask for and to give help to each other.

THE VALIDATING STRATEGIES

Many of the strategies throughout this book incorporate validation. Those on the following pages are especially designed to help us recognize just how lovable and capable we really are.

11

IALAC STRATEGIES

The strategies in this group all help us to appreciate ourselves and each other more. As with the other groups of strategies, they do not have to be done in any particular order.

31. IALAC (I Am Lovable and Capable)
32. Mirror, Mirror
33. Eight Minutes of Validation
34. Classified Ad
35. Proud Whip
36. Symbols of Success
37. Sounds at the Dinner Table
38. Yesterday, Today, and Tomorrow
39. Values Telegrams
40. Hey, Listen!

Strategy 31

*IALAC (I AM LOVABLE AND CAPABLE)**

Each of us wears a sign every day of our lives, although no one can see it or feel it. This sign says, "I am lovable and capable." This is what—deep down—we really know about ourselves,

---

* The story of Randy, a 14-year-old boy whose sign is ripped to shreds in a typical day, is told in Dr. Simon's pamphlet, *I Am Lovable and Capable,* Argus Communications, 1973.

and what we want others to know, too. But because we live in a society that puts people down more than it builds them up, little pieces of our sign constantly keep getting ripped away.

Every time someone snubs us, every time someone says an unkind word to us, every time people we count on let us down, every time we put ourselves down—another little piece of our sign is torn off. By the end of the day, we have little if any of our sign left. But next morning when we wake up and face the world, the sign is whole again.

TIME: When the family will be together for a while—maybe a weekend or holiday morning, or just before dinner when you're spending the evening at home.

PLACE: Home.

EQUIPMENT: An index card, the five-by-eight-inch kind, or large sheet of paper, a straight pin for everyone, Scotch Tape, extra paper.

PROCEDURE: Everyone writes the letters IALAC (we pronounce this *eye-uh-lack*) in the middle of the paper. In the four corners, make jagged lines to symbolize torn paper. (See illustration on page 112.) In the corners write down four things that other people do that *tear* your signs. In the inner sections write down four things other people do that *strengthen* your signs. Then pin your signs to your chests.

Whenever your sign is being torn because of what you or someone else says or does (needling, shouting, hitting, scolding, ridiculing, ignoring), rip off a little piece. When your sign is being strengthened (by compliments, consideration, helpfulness, proud feelings, etc.), tape an extra piece of paper onto it.

After a couple of hours or more, the family comes together and looks at each other's signs. This is a graphic way to demonstrate how your family treats each other. Is there one person everyone else picks on? Is your home atmosphere sign-destroying for everyone? Or are you one of those fortunate families whose signs are bigger at the end of the day than when you started?

FOLLOW-UP: When you come back together again, you might want to ask yourselves some questions:

- Is there anyone whose sign you regularly tear?
- How can you change your behavior toward that person?
- Is there someone who regularly tears your sign?
- What can you do about it?
- Who are the people who regularly add the most pieces to your sign?
- Whose signs do you add to regularly?
- How can you tell someone to stop tearing your sign without tearing their sign?
- What kind of a school would yours be if no one ever tore anyone's sign?
- What can we do to make ours a never-tear-each-other's-sign family?

VARIATIONS:

When company comes to dinner, make each person a place card with the letters IALAC around the name. Just before you begin to eat, explain the meaning of IALAC and ask everyone to tell how someone added to his or her sign on this day.

Each family member makes a small IALAC sign (a square of cardboard attached with a safety pin, a baggage tag hung around a button, or a piece of paper covering a slogan-type button). On a set day, everyone wears the small IALAC sign out on his or her daily rounds. That evening, you all report your day's experiences: how many people asked about the meaning of IALAC, how you answered them, what their reactions were.

Each family member colors half of his/her IALAC sign and wears it (or keeps it with him/her) throughout a typical weekday. The colored half represents the world of the family; the plain half, the world of school or work. Just before bedtime, the family gets together to see which of everyone's two different spheres is more validating. Is your home a refuge from the outside world? Or do the people you are with during the day make you feel better about yourself than your own family does? How can you change the less validating area of your life?

Strategy 32

MIRROR, MIRROR

As hard as it is for most of us to give and take compliments from others, it is usually even harder to give them to and take them from ourselves. Early training in modesty and humility hangs on. We tend to look at ourselves through a distorting mirror that magnifies our faults and minimizes our virtues. This strategy helps to take the distortions out of the mirror and lets us see ourselves as we really are, with all our virtues shining forth.

TIME: Any time when only the immediate family is present.
PLACE: Any private place—around the dinner table, sitting in front of a fireplace, in the car, etc.
EQUIPMENT: None.
PROCEDURE: The starter tells all family members that they will

each have two minutes to talk about things they like about themselves. If people seem hesitant, urge them to talk about anything —looks, skills, deeds, personalities—that might ordinarily be called "bragging."

Everyone listens closely—and then becomes a mirror for everyone else. Each listener tells each speaker at least one admirable thing that the speaker didn't say about him/herself. No put-downs or killer statements are allowed at any time.

This strategy generates a lot of embarrassed giggles, but it also sparks good feelings toward the self and toward other family members.

Strategy 33

EIGHT MINUTES OF VALIDATION

Learning how to validate those we love is like learning how to take pictures. The first time we go out with our little instant camera, we don't know what to photograph. We snap away at everything, without really knowing how to visualize photographs. As we practice our photography, we learn how to use light and shadow, how to notice texture, how to plan compositions.

So it is with compliments. Most of us give only the most obvious ones. We compliment other people so rarely that we never have to go below the surface. But when we validate others on a systematic basis, we make an effort to be more artistic. We look for special facets in people.

As we become more skillful, we would no longer say, for example, "That's a nice dress," but would say instead, "The colors in that dress bring out the beautiful blue of your eyes"—or "The way that dress hangs on your body makes you look like a panther going through the forest." We wouldn't say, "You were a good girl today," but would say instead, "I know how much effort it took for you to be quiet while the baby was taking his nap, and I was really proud of your self-control." Or we might say, "It really means a lot to me when I talk to you and see your brown eyes looking straight at me and I know you're really listening to what I have to say."

TIME: Any time you can spend about twenty uninterrupted minutes together.
PLACE: A room where two family members can be alone.
EQUIPMENT: Two chairs, kitchen timer.
PROCEDURE: First, husband and wife should do this strategy with each other before doing it with the children. (A single parent can do it with a close friend or relative.) Afterward, decide which of you will do it with which children, one at a time.

Pull up two chairs close to each other, or sit on the floor facing each other. Each person takes two minutes to say what she or he likes and appreciates about the other. Then each one takes two minutes to do the same for him/herself. Having to do eight minutes of validation—four for each partner—means that you really have to look for things to validate.

This strategy helps you see things in each other and in yourselves that you have never been aware of before. The pictures that you create will remind you how truly unique and precious are the people you love.

Strategy 34

CLASSIFIED AD

If you have small children, teenagers, or pets, you would appreciate my presence in your house. I get along well with most kids my age and I also have a lot of patience with little kids. I love animals and don't mind taking care of them. I can also serenade you to sleep with my stupendously fantastic piano and flute playing (not both at once, but I'm working on it). Altogether I make a darned good bargain. Just give me a few carrots and I'll be your best friend.

Jenny, 16 years old

Fun-loving, amusing guest. Good at crossword puzzles, laughs at your jokes, doesn't need to be entertained. Ready for walk, biking, swimming, tennis. Can mix any drink and make breakfast. Very neat. Will pitch in to help fix up your place with light carpentry and yard work. Showers daily.

David, 54 years old

When we place a classified ad—to sublet an apartment or sell a house, car, or bicycle—we emphasize the best points of the item offered. We try to make readers feel they will really be missing something if they don't take advantage of this opportunity. Jenny and her father used the same technique on themselves to show other people how lucky they would be to know them.

TIME: Any time.
PLACE: Anywhere you can write.
EQUIPMENT: Paper and pencils.
PROCEDURE: Write a classified ad to rent yourself out for a weekend. Slant your ad for your local newspaper or your favorite magazine. It should be short and snappy and should emphasize some of the reasons why other people would want to have you in their homes for a weekend. Share your ads with each other.

Strategy 35

PROUD WHIP

Pride goeth before destruction, and a haughty spirit before a fall.

—PROVERBS 16:18

A first-grade teacher who had been conducting "Proud Whips" in her classroom every Monday for six weeks was sorry that little

Georgie chose to pass every single time. She never pushed him to participate, though. In the seventh week, near the close of a particularly hectic Monday, Georgie asked, "Aren't you going to do the Proud Whip today?" Ms. Wolf made time for it—and rejoiced with Georgie when he said, "I'm proud that I don't sleep with a night light any more."

Through the years, pride has received a "bad press." People have been cautioned not to be proud for fear of being considered arrogant. Yet two definitions of pride given by Webster's Third New International Dictionary elevate this attribute to something we all need more of. Webster's says pride can be "a sense of delight or elation" and "a sense of one's own worth." This strategy fosters this kind of pride.

TIME: Whenever the family is together, especially when discussing a particular issue.

PLACE: Dinner table, car, around a campfire, etc.

EQUIPMENT: None.

PROCEDURE: The starter asks everyone to think for a minute about what they are proud of in relation to some specific aspect of their lives, or to some particular issue (race relations, ecology, poverty, old people, etc.). Then the starter whips around, calling on everyone. Everyone always has the option of passing. Like Georgie, we may have to wait for the right moment before we participate.

SAMPLE QUESTIONS:

· What did you say or do in the last 24 hours/week/month that you're proud of or happy about?
· What are you proud of in relation to . . .
> a friend?
> your family?
> money?
> school?
> helping someone else?
> understanding between people of different races?
> your religion?

- What are you proud of that you can do on your own?
- What new skill are you proud of?
- Are you proud of a time when you showed courage, but not in a physical sense?
- Are you proud of a time when you showed physical courage?
- Are you proud of . . .
    a job you did that was hard to do?
    something that you really worked hard to improve?
    something you made yourself?
    a fear you've overcome?
    a bad habit you've overcome?
    something you've done that's beautiful?
    something funny?
    a way you helped keep your city/school/home clean?
    a gift you gave someone?
- Are you proud of something you've done for . . .
    an older person?
    a smaller child?
    a sick person?
    a poor person?
    a friend?

We need to be proud of achievements that attest to our competence, deeds that prove our virtue, personality traits we have worked hard to cultivate, aspects of our lives we enjoy basking in. Pride in this sense is a cherishing of something in our life. The more things we feel good about, the better we feel about ourselves. The more we recognize which beliefs and actions make us proud, the easier it is for us to live value-filled lives. The Proud Whip helps us do this.

Strategy 36

SYMBOLS OF SUCCESS

During the 1960s, the senior author, an activist in the civil rights movement, was asked to help rebuild a bombed-out Mississippi church. Since I feared for my life, I hesitated, but finally decided that I valued equal rights so much that—for my own sake—I would have to take the risks involved. When I came home, I brought back a lump of glass that had been melted out of shape in the original explosion at the church. This lump of glass now sits on my desk. It symbolizes a success in my life, a time when I wrestled with my fears and did what I felt was the right thing.

Most of us surround ourselves with symbols of our successes. These symbols may be trophies, framed certificates, photos of ourselves in significant situations. Or—like that lump of glass—they may be symbols that have unique, special meanings. Thinking about the success symbols that matter and why they are important helps us to know just what we value.

TIME: Any time.

PLACE: Anywhere.

EQUIPMENT: None.

PROCEDURE: Everyone describes one symbol of success on display in an office, bedroom, or other place where she or he hopes that others will notice and comment on it. After everyone has spoken, pose questions like the following:

- How do you feel when someone comes in and fails to notice your success symbol?
- If someone does not notice, does your feeling about that person change?
- Has anyone ever made fun of or put down your symbol? If so, what happened to your relationship with that person?
- Are you embarrassed when people ask you about your symbol, or do you enjoy talking about it?

· If a good friend asked to borrow your symbol, would you lend it out? If you did, and if the symbol were lost, what would happen to the friendship?
· Do you think this symbol will be important to you a year from now? Five years from now? All your life?

Strategy 37

SOUNDS AT THE DINNER TABLE

What does your family sound like at the dinner table? Does constant squabbling accompany every meal? Is the room silent as everyone rushes through to finish eating and leave? Does conversation go on only between mother and father, while the children eat silently in boredom? Is the talk usually a potpourri of small talk, unimportant questions, and "pass the peas"? Or is the hour meaningful for both individual and family growth?

TIME: Dinnertime.
PLACE: Dinner table.
EQUIPMENT: Tape recorder, cassette.
PROCEDURE: To preserve the maximum degree of spontaneity, it is best if one person can plug in the tape recorder without saying anything to the other family members. (This person must erase the tape later if anyone objects to its being kept.) Even if people are aware that the recorder is on, though, they usually forget about it within a few minutes and behave and talk normally.

After thirty minutes, play the tape for your family. Chances are, you'll all get some surprises: "Is that *me*?" "Did *I* say *that*?" "Boy, do you sound *mean*!" "What a boring conversation!"

People are usually fascinated to hear themselves on tape, even though they may be dismayed by what they hear themselves saying. This strategy tends to spark interesting and helpful discussions about ways that family members can relate to each other. It often leads to such resolutions as "No killer statements," "No put-downs," "No self-put-downs," and so forth. It may also inspire you to make your dinnertimes more interesting by using more values whips, encouraging everyone to talk about high points, stimulating people to bring provocative questions to the table along with their appetites.

Strategy 38

YESTERDAY, TODAY, AND TOMORROW

Our lives are made up of one day after another. They can either "creep in this petty pace from day to day" as they did for Macbeth, or they can be "of cheerful yesterdays/And confident tomorrows" as for the man in the Wordsworth poem. This strategy helps us to analyze just what our days do hold for us, what we would like them to hold for us, and how we can make our dreams come true.

TIME: Any time.
PLACE: Anywhere you can write.
EQUIPMENT: Paper and pencils.
PROCEDURE: The starter asks the following six questions. Everyone writes down a brief answer to each. Afterward, family members share their answers with each other.
THE QUESTIONS:

1. What is one thing you love about your yesterdays?
2. What is one thing you love about your today?
3. What is one thing your tomorrows hold for you?
4. What part of your today do you want in your tomorrow?
5. What part of yesterday do you want to take to your tomorrow?
6. What is one thing that you can do to take the best of today or yesterday to your tomorrow?

Strategy 39
VALUES TELEGRAMS

The arrival of the Western Union messenger used to signal important events in people's lives. Even today, when telegrams are usually delivered by telephone, they convey a sense of urgency and significance.

All of us have many important messages that we don't send. But it is important to let other people know how we feel, what matters to us, what we appreciate about them, and what we want from them. It is important to send messages both to those close to us and to those who serve us in some official capacity.

Putting our thoughts in writing tends to give them a solidity and impact that the spoken word sometimes misses. Yet many people don't write down how they feel because the very act of writing scares them. Confining a message to a brief telegram style makes it easier. This strategy focuses on two types of values telegrams, those that validate other people and those that urge them to do something.

TIME: Any time.

PLACE: Anywhere you can write.

EQUIPMENT: Pencils and six three-by-five-inch cards or six telegram blanks for each person.

PROCEDURE:

Part One: Validation Telegrams

Think of three people: 1) someone in your immediate family, 2) someone in your personal life, and 3) someone in public life. Think about what you admire in each of these people— some personality trait, some action they have taken, some aspect of the way they lead their lives.

Compose a brief message (try to stay under twenty-five words) of validation for each of these people.

Share your telegrams with each other.

Be sure to send the telegrams out within the week.

Part Two: Action Telegrams

Again, think of three people: 1) someone in the immediate family, 2) someone in your personal life, and 3) someone in public life. Think about one thing you would like each of them to do. Do you want the public person to perform some values-related action? Do you want the people in your private life to change their attitudes or actions to make their lives better? Keep your messages warm and caring.

Share these messages.

Send them out within the week (not necessarily as formal telegrams).

FOLLOW-UP: Plan to get together once a month to ask yourselves, "Whom do I want to validate?" "Whom do I want action from?" By sending messages this way, you will probably find that you are communicating feelings that otherwise would go unsaid.

SAMPLE TELEGRAMS (to use as illustration)

Validation:

TO MOM: I WANT YOU TO KNOW HOW GRATEFUL I AM FOR YOUR STRENGTH AND HELP TO ME WHEN DAD DIED. LOVE, KATHY

TO JAMIE: I APPRECIATE THE WAY YOU REACHED OUT TO YOUR SISTER WHEN SHE NEEDED SOMEONE TO TALK TO. YOU SHOWED A LOT OF SENSITIVITY. LOVE, MOTHER

TO MOLLY: WE WANT YOU TO KNOW THAT EVEN IF YOU DON'T PURSUE YOUR MUSIC PROFESSIONALLY, WE APPRECIATE THE WAY YOU HAVE ENRICHED OUR LIVES BY FILLING OUR HOUSE WITH BEAUTIFUL MUSIC. LOVE, MOTHER AND DAD

TO DAVID: THANK YOU FOR ALWAYS BEING WILLING TO INTERRUPT YOUR WORK TO LISTEN TO WHAT IS ON MY MIND. LOVE, SARA ROSE

TO CEZAR CHAVEZ: YOUR COURAGE AND PERSISTENCE HAVE MADE LIFE BETTER FOR THOUSANDS OF FARMWORKERS AND THEIR FAMILIES. WE ARE GRATEFUL. THE RIVERA FAMILY

Action:

TO PHILIP: I URGE YOU NOT TO WORRY ABOUT ALWAYS COMING IN FIRST. WE'LL LOVE YOU EVEN IF YOU'RE SECOND OR THIRD OR FOURTH. LOVE, DADDY

TO STEPHANIE: I URGE YOU NOT TO PUT YOURSELF DOWN SO MUCH. YOU ARE LOVABLE AND CAPABLE AND BEAUTIFUL, TOO. LOVE, MOMMY

TO DADDY: I URGE YOU TO GIVE UP SMOKING. I LOVE YOU SO MUCH THAT I WANT YOU TO BE AROUND FOR A LONG, LONG TIME. LOVE, RICHARD

TO SENATOR WOLFF: I URGE YOU TO VOTE FOR THE BILL MAKING STRIP MINING ILLEGAL SO WE CAN SAVE WHAT'S LEFT OF OUR BEAUTIFUL APPALACHIAN HILLS. YOUR CONSTITUENT, JANE DOE

Strategy 40

HEY, LISTEN!

Through this three-part strategy, we learn how to listen to each other by seeing in a dramatic way how we often do *not* listen.

TIME: Any time. The three parts of the strategy may be done in one long session or on three consecutive days.
PLACE: A room or area that's big enough to allow people to separate into groups of two or three.
EQUIPMENT: Kitchen timer.
PROCEDURE: One person in each group of two or three is the first focus person. When that person speaks, the others focus their attention upon him/her. The focus person is given one minute to tell the story of his/her life and some of the most important events in it.

Part One: "Tuning Out"
   The other people in the group are instructed, within the focus person's hearing, *not* to listen to him or her. While she or he is

talking, the others are to talk to each other, look out the window, read something—anything short of getting up and walking away. Everyone gets a turn at being the focus person.

Afterward, all participants tell how they felt while trying to tell their stories. People usually express feelings of frustration, anger, and a feeling of inadequacy that they were not able to hold the interest of their non-listeners, even though they know that the other people were only following instructions. This can lead into a discussion of all the times in our daily lives when we feel people aren't paying attention to what we have to say—or when we find that we aren't listening to others.

Part Two: "Hooking On"

This time the other people *seem* to be listening to the focus person. But they keep interrupting to "hook" their own statements to those made by the focus person.

The focus person might begin: "I was born in Pittsburgh, and we moved from there when I was three . . ." Someone might interrupt with, "I was in Pittsburgh once. It's really dirty. I hate dirty cities, don't you?" Another might add, "Oh, but it's not dirty any more. They have that beautiful Golden Triangle area now. It's wonderful what they can do with an old city." All of this could be appropriate in a discussion about urban renewal, but it is completely irrelevant to the focus person's life story.

After all have taken their turns and then described their feelings while the others were "hooking on," a discussion may take place about this type of non-listening. It is even more common than the first kind, subtler, and harder to deal with. How many of us are guilty of it? How do we react when others do it to us?

Part Three: "Zeroing In"

Finally we get to hear everyone's one-minute autobiography. All family members concentrate on listening to the focus person. Afterward, everyone may ask one question relating to the focus person's feelings about what she or he has just said. Then the focus person contrasts the way she or he felt during this part of the strategy with her or his feelings during the first two parts.

12

VALUES CLARIFICATION IN EVERYDAY FAMILY LIFE

In a home that embraces the principles of Values Clarification, everyone—from the tiniest baby on up—is respected as a valuable person. On issues of importance to the whole family, everyone's opinion is sought. As a matter of course in everyday life, everyone's feelings are considered. The parents do not rule by divine right. They recognize that they have to enforce certain decisions, sometimes unpopular, because their accumulated life experience and careful thought have convinced them that they are right. Since they give careful thought to their decisions, they are always willing to explain their reasons.

Such parents recognize that even small children can come up with fresh insights, good ideas, new ways to solve family problems. So they encourage their children to help decide such matters as family outings, vacations, household chores, extracurricular activities, clothing purchases, and the resolution of conflicts.

Children can be involved to some degree in most family decisions. Suppose Mr. and Mrs. Abrams decide to move to another city for professional advancement. They recognize that the move will disrupt their children's lives. They don't dismiss the youngsters' concerns about leaving friends and familiar surroundings by saying, "Oh, you'll learn to love it. Look how fast you got used to it here! And besides, you're always fighting with your friends—you'll never miss them!" Instead, they ask their children, "What can we do to make this move easier for you?"

Jenny may ask for a room "just as big as the one I have now." Nancy may want one "all to myself." Dorie may ask to come back to see her old friends for the first few months after the move. Whenever possible, we should encourage our children to see the positive things we can do to make life better—the ways we can improve any situation. We don't always have to "take our lumps"; we can learn how to make life smoother.

In a values-oriented home, many parental decisions are open to negotiation. When children don't like a decision, they can question it. One weekend the Simon family had planned to go to their farm in the Adirondacks, but 14-year-old Juliana wanted to spend time in town with her boyfriend. Since a songfest had been planned and guests invited, her parents felt they needed her at the farm. "I was starting to get uptight and rigid and insist she go with us," says her father, "when Juliana said, 'Wait a minute—can't we come up with some alternative?' " The negotiated solution allowed Juliana to stay in town one day, sleep at a neighbor's house, and take an early-morning bus up to the farm to be there in time for the big sing. This was an alternative everyone could accept.

Parents who help their children clarify values don't say, "You have to do this because I said so." An answer like that discourages an open exchange of feelings. It also thwarts the search for alternative solutions—a search that can serve us well all our lives in all sorts of situations.

The constantly questioning attitude implicit in the Values Clarification approach lifts some of the burden from parents to be absolute paragons of virtue and absolute fountains of wisdom. We know that our actions are not always in accord with our beliefs. We know we don't have all the answers. We don't pretend we do.

Parents worry about being consistent with children. We teach them to tell the truth, and then they catch us in a lie. What can we do? We can be defensive and say, "You'll understand when you're older," or we can explain why we felt this lie was kinder than the truth. Or we can use the Values Clarification approach and ask, "What else do you think I could have done?" "How else could I have handled this situation?" "What would have happened if I had told the truth?" "What do you think I should do next time?" Thus, our children learn to appreciate the complexity of many issues, and we learn to question ourselves in a constructive way.

13

GETTING TO KNOW YOUR FAMILY

After doing Strategy 1, My Favorite Things (see page 34), 15-year-old Marty said, "I realized, after trying to figure out which of the things on my list my parents would also have had on theirs, that I really don't know my mother and father very well. I'm going to try to get to know them better."

Most of us don't know our families well. If someone asked you, "What have been the most significant experiences in your children's lives?" would you feel confident that you know the answer? If someone asked your children, "Which people have had the greatest influence on your parents?" could they venture a guess? Do you know each other's cherished dreams? Do you know which values you all hold? Do brothers and sisters really know each other?

Most of us live in a rushed and hectic world. Between the children's music lessons and basketball practice and Sunday school and our own jobs and meetings and social lives, we tend to live by the clock. We do things the most practical and efficient way. But practicality and efficiency are not always conducive to welding close, warm family relationships.

Furthermore, in this age of individuality, we often encourage our children all to "do their own thing." Too often the family members are all so busy pursuing their own interests, activities, and friends that they hardly see each other, much less get to know and enjoy each other as people.

Many persons don't get to know and be close to their brothers and sisters until they grow up, sometimes not until they all have families of their own. These are the fortunate ones. Many siblings never understand or feel close to each other as long as they live.

But how marvelous it can be to get to know and trust a brother or sister! Friends may often be closer than brothers and sisters— but friendships wax and wane, whereas a sister is a sister for the rest of one's life. Our siblings understand in a very special, deep way why we are who we are.

In some lucky families, parents and children enjoy doing things together, develop special family rituals that they all look forward to, like each other's company, and respect each other. The strategies in the next section can help *your* family reach some of these goals. They can help you get to know each other better, respect and understand each other, and become closer. Through the questions you ask and the topics you explore, your children can see where your values come from. And you can see what's important to them. The family is bound to grow in mutual understanding.

14

STRATEGIES FOR GETTING TO KNOW THE ONES WE LOVE

The emphasis in this group of strategies is on understanding the feelings, attitudes, beliefs, and values of the members of our own families. As we are open with each other and disclose ourselves to each other, we deepen mutual trust and love.

41. Family Coat of Arms
42. Family Interview
43. Support
44. Board of Directors
45. People in My World
46. Privacy Pond
47. Dare I?
48. Drawing the Line
49. Family Bulletin Board
50. This Is Your Life (Your Own Monopoly Game)
51. Show and Talk
52. What's Important?

Strategy 41

FAMILY COAT OF ARMS

Like the Personal Coat of Arms (see page 81), the Family Coat of Arms is much more intriguing than any emblem of any royal family ever could be. It symbolizes your own family and some of the things you want to say about it.

TIME: Any time the family is all together.
PLACE: Anywhere you can write.
EQUIPMENT: Large sheets of paper and pencils.
PROCEDURE: Everyone draws an outline of a coat of arms (see page 133), divides it and numbers it as shown. Answer the first five questions below with drawings, and the sixth with words. And remember—the quality of the artwork doesn't count, only the meaning behind it.
THE QUESTIONS:

1. What do you consider our family's greatest achievement?
2. What is one special thing you admire about each member?
3. What three family activities do you enjoy doing?
4. What one thing could other family members do to make you happy?
5. What one thing should our family try to improve?
6. What three words represent how you would like your family to think of you?

Family members then share their coats of arms with each other, covering any drawings they want to keep private and explaining the others in any way they wish.
VARIATIONS: You may substitute different questions for any of the six above, such as:

3. What three family rituals mean a lot to you?

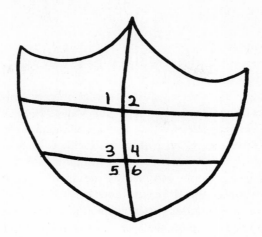

5. What is something that our family has improved over the past two years?
6. What could be a family motto that we could all believe in? Write out three separate words or a short sentence.

Through this strategy and the discussion following it, you are likely to grasp some feelings that family members may never have expressed before.

FOLLOW-UP: Everyone may wish to make an "Ah-hah!" statement (see page 49) about what she or he learned about the family: "I learned that our family . . ."

Strategy 42

FAMILY INTERVIEW

We want to know so much about each other. Yet how rarely we ask the questions that would yield the answers we seek! This strategy helps family members raise these questions in an atmosphere of safety.

TIME: Any time.

PLACE: Some place where the family has privacy.

EQUIPMENT: None.

PROCEDURE: One person volunteers to be interviewed first. She or he picks a topic from the list of Ten Values-Rich Areas (see below). Everyone else may ask two questions involving the interviewee's personal beliefs, attitudes, feelings, or actions relating to this topic. The interviewee is in control of this strategy. She/he calls on people and has the option of choosing not to answer any question. If she/he does answer, though, she/he must tell the truth. After the inteview, the interviewee can ask anyone else any questions that she/he has already answered. All answers are accepted as given, with no judgments or arguments.

TEN VALUES-RICH AREAS:

Family	Religion
Self	Leisure
Friendship	Money
Society	Work and School
Morals and Ethics	Love and Sexuality

SAMPLE INTERVIEW QUESTIONS:

· Who is the meanest kid you know?
· Do you plan to send any Valentines this year?
· Who is the nicest grown-up or child you know not in your immediate family? What does she or he do to make you like him or her?
· Why do you think your friends like you?
· Have you ever felt as if you had no friends?
· Did you ever receive a love letter?
· Did you ever write a love letter?
· Are you happy you're the sex you are? Have you ever wished you could be of the opposite sex?
· Do you sometimes feel uncomfortable talking to boys/girls?

- What was the nicest present you ever gave a family member?
- Of all the things your family does together, which is the most fun?
- What do you think you will do about your parents when they get old?
- Have you ever been ashamed of anyone in your family?
- In what ways would you bring up your children differently from the way you're being raised?
- Have you ever wished you were an only child?
- Do you wish you could live forever?
- Why did you cry the last time?
- What is your favorite dessert?
- Have you ever wished you were older or younger than you are now?
- Have you ever wished you could be something else other than a human?
- What scares you the most?
- What really gets you mad?
- Will you smoke cigarettes when you grow up?
- What toy do you think you'll always remember?
- Which TV show do you think is stupid?
- What sport would you like to be better at?
- What is your favorite book?
- What would you do with your time if there were no TV?
- When did you hold the most money in your hand?
- Can you think of two things you could do to help your family save money?
- If someone gave you five dollars, would you spend it or save it? What would you spend it on or save it for?
- What is the hardest chore you do around the house?
- What are/were you best in in school?
- How do you deal with unpleasant aspects of school or work?
- Have you ever felt bad because someone was better at something?
- Where have you been where they have the most trees?
- As you look at the world around you, what is something you sometimes wonder about?

· Have you ever found out that someone you trusted lied to you?
· Do you think you could ever kill another person? In what circumstances?
· Have you ever cheated on a test?
· What do you think about in church or temple?
· What do you like best about practicing your religion?

The questions that people can ask in these interviews are, of course, endless, limited only by their genuine interest in what makes each other tick. The answers reward all the participants by yielding precious knowledge about other family members. But the interviewees probably gain most of all, because as they are answering questions they may never have considered before, they are learning about themselves.

Strategy 43

SUPPORT

One of the hardest things in many families is to understand each other's point of view. "How can you stand to listen to that awful noise—you call *that* music?" "Well, just because we are Jewish, I don't see why we can't have a Christmas tree!" "So what if I'm late for school? I get all my work done." "Boy, Dad, haven't you *ever* worn a beard?"

"Role-playing," or putting oneself in another person's place, is a technique that works well in all sorts of situations. This strategy carries it a step further.

TIME: Any time the family is together, especially during a hot and heavy argument.
PLACE: Anywhere.
EQUIPMENT: None.

PROCEDURE: One person makes a statement about any issue, and then everyone else makes one—and only one—statement *in support* of the first speaker's position. So when Josh, 5, said, "Everybody should be allowed to eat as much candy as they want," his mother bit back the urge to explain why too much candy was bad for him. Instead, she said, "Probably nobody has ever had a chance to eat all the candy they really want. Everyone should be able to sit down at least once in a lifetime and eat two or three pounds at a sitting if that's what you really want to do."

And Father said, "Well, variety's the spice of life. The chance to eat one of every kind of candy bar, hard candy, and chewy candy ever made sure could bring a lot of variety into a person's life."

The more people disagree with the original statement, the more creative they will have to be with their statements of support. And the better they may all end up understanding each other.

SAMPLE STATEMENTS:

· Kids should be allowed to stay up as late as they want.
· Turning your homework in on time is very important.
· Nobody should take a bath more than once a week.
· It's silly to wait till you get married to have sexual intercourse.
· Mothers should not work outside the house.
· Boys should wear their hair short.
· Girls shouldn't wear jeans to school.
· Parents should never spank kids.
· School is a waste of time.
· Children shouldn't talk back to their elders.
· People of different races should live with their own kind.
· Children are better off in day-care centers than home.

Having to come up with an argument for an opposing point of view helps people to realize that every issue has more than one side. The game helps people to see the reasonableness of other people's points of view, although it makes no effort to try to get people to sympathize or empathize with them.

Strategy 44

BOARD OF DIRECTORS

Think of your life as if it were a large organization—a rich corporation or a powerful association, for example. It is complicated to manage. Its activities require many daily decisions, for which several people often share the responsibility. It is run by a Board of Directors, a group of people who have an overall understanding of the organization and are expert in the various skills needed to run it. The board works under the direction of a chairperson, who ultimately casts deciding votes.

Chances are that you, as the chairperson of your .life, call upon an active Board of Directors to help you in running it. Your board is composed of those people who influence or control your life to some degree. In our youth our actions are guided largely by other people. Then at some point in our lives, most of us assume the major responsibility for our lives. Yet we still may call on our board members for advice and opinions. How does your personal Board of Directors operate?

TIME: Any time teenagers and adults are together; this strategy is too sophisticated for most younger children.
PLACE: Anywhere you can write.
EQUIPMENT: Paper and pencils.
PROCEDURE: Draw a large rectangle. At one end draw a circle to represent you, the Chairperson of the Board. On each of the long sides of the table draw three circles. Write in them the names or initials of six people who sit on the Board of Directors of your life. These are people who are important to you; those whom you would ask for advice, or who impose their opinions on you without being asked. In any case, they influence your decisions and the way you live your life. If you have more than six, draw more circles; if fewer, leave some blank.
Code these directors as follows:

- Put a "+" by those that you're glad to have on your Board.
- Put a "−" by those you would be happy to see resign.
- Put a "0" by those about whom you're not sure.
- Put "TB" by those whom you serve by being on *their* Boards.

At the empty end of the table, draw three circles. These represent consultants who offer advice in special areas of concern—a gym coach, a guidance counselor, a teacher, a psychotherapist, for example. Write in the names or initials in these circles.

Look at your board table and think about whether you are chairperson of your board. Do you have free choice? Are you open to all your board members, able to listen to their opinions, able to weigh them, and then able to make your decisions according to what *you* think best? If you are your own chairperson, think about the circumstances when you first realized that you were in charge. Was it sudden or gradual? Write a key word for your first take-charge underneath your circle—"college," for example.

Have you ever temporarily resigned as chairperson? If so, put a star by the person who took over for you. Put a "−" or "+", depending on how well that person served you.

Would you like to replace any of your board members? Why? Which ones? How can you do this?

Write an "Ah-hah!" statement about what you have learned about your life from doing this strategy.

FOLLOW-UP: Draw another board table. Write in the names of the people who sat on your board when you were 8 years old. How many of them are still on your board? Are they as important now as they were then?

Draw another board table. Write in the names of those who sat on your board when you were 18 years old. Compare that board with your present board.

The family that shares information gleaned from this strategy will most likely learn more about themselves and each other in one evening than they could have dreamed possible. But you have to be careful. Since this strategy delves into sensitive areas of family relationships, it is especially important to safeguard everyone's privacy. No one should be pressured to talk about his or her Board of Directors. Even if you all keep your information to yourselves, valuable learning will have taken place.

Strategy 45

PEOPLE IN MY WORLD

Our values are intertwined with the people we have relationships with—our families, our sweethearts, our friends, our neighbors, our teachers, our colleagues. The way we feel and act toward them reveals the standards that are important to us. This strategy helps us identify the people who are most important to us and how they affect our lives.

TIME: Any time.

PLACE: Anywhere you can write.

EQUIPMENT: Large sheets of paper and pencils of two different colors for each participant.

PROCEDURE: Everyone draws a large circle in the center of the paper. Write your initials in the circle. This represents you. Surrounding this circle, draw in all the people important to you, using triangles for males and circles for females, one color for family members and a second color for non-relatives. Write in the initials for each person. (See drawing on page 141.) Show the intensity of the relationship by the size of the shapes and by the distance that you place them from yourself.

Draw lines between yourself and the others. If you think you feel more strongly toward the other person than that person feels toward you, make an arrow pointing toward the other person. If the reverse is true, point the arrow toward yourself. If the relationship is mutual, put arrows at each end.

Put a "2" by those people with whom your relationship is dif-

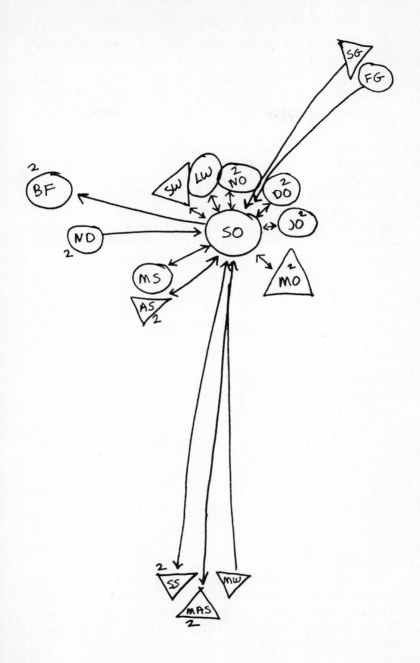

ferent now from what it was two years ago. Think about the way in which it has changed.

Examine the patterns that have emerged, and write out an "Ah-hah!" statement about what you have just learned about yourself and your relationships. Share your statements with each other.

FOLLOW-UP: Pick the three people who are most important in your life. List three things that each one of these three people wants you to do, to be, or to value.

Circle the things that you also want for yourself.

Everyone takes two minutes to tell how you deal with those situations when what *you* want conflicts with what someone *wants* you to want.

Strategy 46

PRIVACY POND

Suppose you received a public award that you didn't deserve because you had cheated to get it? Suppose someone in your family was in an institution for the emotionally ill? Suppose you had voted for a President who turned out to be a criminal? Suppose you did better on a test than anyone else in your class? To whom would you tell these things? Everyone you know? No one? A trusted confidante?

Imagine your life as a pond of water, with you as a pebble tossed into its middle. You are the very center of your life; everything else revolves around you. And everyone in your life fits into one of the ever-widening circles that spread out from the center.

How transparent are the waters of your life underneath all these circles? How much of yourself do you reveal at each level of relationship? What kinds of things do you consider most private? What are you most willing to share? The "Privacy Pond" helps you find out.

TIME: Any time.

PLACE: Anywhere you can write.

EQUIPMENT: Large sheets of paper and pencils.

PROCEDURE: Everyone draws a series of five concentric circles. The smallest one represents you; write your initials and put a tiny dot in the center. The dot represents that information about yourself that even you don't have. The circle itself represents those things about yourself that you would not tell anyone else in the whole world.

The second circle represents such intimate, trusted people as your best friend or your husband or wife—a person or persons with whom you can share *almost* everything. In this circle, write the names or initials of the two people you trust the most with your secrets.

The third circle is made up of people you feel close to, to a slightly lesser degree—these are friends, siblings, family members—to whom you would trust some knowledge about yourself. In this circle, write the names of four of your next closest friends or relatives.

In the circle surrounding this are all the other people you know—your acquaintances at school or work or neighborhood —all those people whose lives touch yours only slightly. In this circle write the initials of eight people whom you sometimes talk to.

The outer ring represents all the strangers you may meet once, and will never see again. Leave this one blank.

The starter then asks everyone to think about the following statements. If these applied to you, with whom would you share them? As each item is read, everyone writes down the key word in the appropriate circle:

· How much money you (or your parents) earned last year (key word: income)
· Your masturbation experiences (masturbation)
· That you once read someone else's diary or personal letter without permission (diary)
· Whom you plan to vote for in the next election (vote)

- That you love one of your parents (or children) more than another (favorite)
- That you cheated in a test (cheat)
- That you stole something (stole)
- That you hit a small child with your car (car)
- Your favorite food (food)
- Your favorite daydream (daydream)
- That you're afraid to be alone at night in a big house (alone)
- That one of your parents is an alcoholic (alcoholic)
- How much you weigh (weigh)
- What you eat for breakfast (breakfast)
- How old you are (age)
- That your father spent a year in jail (jail)
- That you once attempted suicide (suicide)
- That you drank so much you passed out (drunk)
- That you have taken illegal drugs (drugs)
- That you're afraid to ride in an elevator (phobia)
- About something you're really good at (brag)
- That you lied in a court of law (lied)
- That you have an illness you know you'll die from (die)
- That you are ashamed of your parents (parents)
- That you have a birthmark (birthmark)

After you have all written down your answers, look at the words in your circles and try to find patterns. Write an "Ah-hah!" statement about what you've learned about yourself.

FOLLOW-UP: These questions can lead to a stimulating family discussion:

- Do you consider yourself a very private or a very open person?
- Are there certain subjects (sex, money, morals, etc.) about which you are more private than others?
- Would you like to be more open?
- Do you regret having told certain things to other people?
- Were you surprised to find that there are some things you might share with strangers that you wouldn't share with your close friends? Why do you suppose that is?
- Do you think your intimates know things about you that you

don't know about yourself? How could you find out those things?
· What kinds of risks are involved with being too open?
· What kinds of risks are involved with being too closed?
· Can you think of times when publicly stating a value or sharing private information can have harmful results?

Each of us needs to know what we feel is right for us to share with people in all of our privacy circles. This strategy helps us to get in touch with our feelings of trust in other people and our feelings about the kinds of things we need to keep to ourselves.

We also need to recognize those times when public affirmation of a value may work against some other value. Suppose, for example, a member of your family is an alcoholic. You may want other people to recognize alcoholism as an illness rather than a moral failure. You may feel that being publicly open about alcoholism is the best way to do this. But your relative has sworn the family to secrecy. If you talk publicly about his alcoholism, you will be betraying his confidence, embarrassing him, and possibly even endangering his livelihood. You are caught in a values conflict, in which you have to choose one value over another.

So even though public affirmation is one of the Seven Steps to Values, there may be times in your life when you cannot apply it, even to what is in every other respect a deeply held value.

Strategy 47

DARE I?

Life holds all sort of risks—physical, as when we ski down a steep slope; intellectual, as when we sign up for a difficult course; and emotional, as when we tell someone we love him or her.

People who are afraid of all risks cannot walk outside their front door, have an intimate relationship, or learn something new. People who take too many risks often end up maimed and battered, physically and emotionally. What then is the right amount of risk? How does each of us handle risk-taking? How can we give ourselves courage to take more risks—or tone down our tendency to take too many?

TIME: Any time.
PLACE: Any place you can write.
EQUIPMENT: Pencils and paper.
PROCEDURE:
Part One: Everyone numbers from 1 to 20 on a sheet of paper. The starter announces, "I will read out twenty risks. Write a key word next to each number. If you would *never* take the risk, write 'N' next to the number. If it is a risk you would take *almost always,* write 'A' next to it. If you might take it *sometimes,* write 'S,' and think about what might lead you to take it or discourage you from taking it. If the risk is not applicable in your life, put an 'X.' "
The Twenty Risks

1. Trying out for the lead in the school play (Key word: play)
2. Not studying before a math test (math)
3. Going up to someone of the opposite sex and telling him/her you'd like to get to know him/her better. (know)
4. Riding a motorcycle without a helmet (helmet)
5. Riding a bicycle after dark without a light (bike)
6. Smoking marijuana (pot)
7. Stealing something (stealing)
8. Sitting in the front seat of a car without wearing a seat belt (belt)
9. Diving off a high board (diving)
10. Calling up a friend you know is angry with you and asking her/him why (angry)

11. Going door-to-door in your neighborhood to try to get some baby-sitting jobs (door)
12. Sniffing cocaine (coke)
13. Going skating when the pond is not officially open (skate)
14. Playing on the railroad tracks (track)
15. Telling your teacher she/he just told the class something you know is wrong (teacher)
16. Calling up a friend who's having a party and asking why you weren't invited (party)
17. Raising your hand in class when you *think* you know the answer but you're not sure (hand)
18. Trying out a new recipe on guests (recipe)
19. Telling your boss you'll quit if you don't get the raise you want (raise)
20. Flying with a friend who's piloting his/her own small plane (plane)

Part Two: Each person makes an "Ah-hah!" statement about the risks in his or her life.

Part Three: Family members share their answers to the twenty risks, always reserving the right to pass. As each person explains why she or he would or would not take a certain risk, you understand each other better and reflect on your own attitudes.

VARIATIONS:

Risk Whip—Everyone answers, "What's one risk you took during the past week? How do you feel about the outcome?" Everyone gets two minutes to talk.

Everyone writes down all the risks she or he took in the past week, puts a plus by the ones that turned out well and a minus by those that turned out badly, and then answers, "If you had known the outcome in advance, what might you have done differently?"

You each make your own list of twenty risks, which can be as commonplace as crossing the street or as adventuresome as climbing Mount Everest. They could include:

Five risks that you take as part of your everyday life
Five risks that you don't have to take but want to take to get
something
Five risks that you wouldn't take under any circumstances
Five risks that have changed your life or could do so

Strategy 48

DRAWING THE LINE

"No, sir! That's where I draw the line!" A common enough
statement—but what does it really mean? Most of us have
many places where we draw the line. This is a point we can't
be pushed beyond. As you explore the lines you draw in your
own life and look for the reasons behind your stands, you may
discover values you never realized you had.

TIME: Any time.
PLACE: Anywhere.
EQUIPMENT: None.
PROCEDURE: Starter poses a question like those listed below. All
family members answer, "whip"-style. After everyone has given
a brief answer, you all explain the reasons behind your answers.
SAMPLE QUESTIONS:
Where would you draw the line on . . .

how old people have to be before they can . . .

   vote
   drink beer
   live away from their parents
   be treated as an adult in the courts
   be President of the United States
   quit school

marry
drink coffee?

how much money . . .

- a candidate for office should be permitted to spend on his or her campaign?
- you would spend on a movie?
- you would lend to a friend?
- people should be allowed to earn without paying any income tax?
- people should be allowed to earn and still get help from welfare?
- a 6-year-old's allowance should be?
- a 16-year-old's allowance should be?

Where would you draw the line on . . .

- how long you will wait in line to see a movie?
- how much TV a 5-year-old should be allowed to watch?
- how late an 8-year-old can stay up on school nights?
- how old people should be before they go out on dates?
- how far a 10-year-old should live from school to ride the bus?
- how bad a crime has to be to be punished with death?
- what another country would do that would make you declare war?
- how long a teenager's telephone conversations can last?
- at what age people should pay for their own phones?
- how late you will wait for someone who is late for an appointment?
- how late someone can come to a party without your getting angry?
- how overcooked you will tolerate corn on the cob?
- how many times a friend gives away a confidence before you lose trust in that person?
- what kind of hand-me-down clothes you will not wear?
- how long clothing hangs in your closet unworn before you give it away?

Where would you draw the line on how long (in days, weeks or months) you could get along without . . .

> telephone
> electricity
> records
> radio
> validation
> television
> air conditioning
> mail
> touching
> seeing other people?

Strategy 49

FAMILY BULLETIN BOARD

Every family could benefit from having a bulletin board in a place where everyone sees it every day. Aside from being a perfect place to leave messages ("I'll be home late—please start dinner"), it's an ideal pump-primer for other kinds of communication.

TIME: Any time.

PLACE: Anywhere.

EQUIPMENT: Bulletin board, straight pins or tacks (may be a metal surface like the front of the refrigerator, with a set of magnets to attach items).

PROCEDURE: Everyone is encouraged to regularly post poems, quotations, song lyrics, cartoons, photos, newspaper clippings, and other items that provide food for thought for family conversations. When the family gets together—at dinner and at other times—people take turns choosing which bulletin-board items to talk about.

Strategy 50

THIS IS YOUR LIFE

If your family likes to play Monopoly, you'll love this strategy. It operates somewhat like the classic board game but is custom-tailored to you and your family.

TIME: This requires a *lot* of time, so start it when you'll have at least a couple of hours or more to spend.

PLACE: Any room where you can spread out on either the floor or a large table.

EQUIPMENT: Monopoly game, a sheet of oaktag from a stationery or an art supply store, pencils, crayons or paints, scissors, paper, markers.

PROCEDURE: Cut the oaktag to the same size as the board from the Monopoly game, and mark out squares for streets, special properties, etc. But instead of copying the Monopoly board, insert items meaningful to your family. Give the streets on your board the names of streets in your town. In place of the railroads, utility companies, jail, etc., put in special places in your family's life—your children's school, your church or temple, your place of work, Grandma's house, the local movie theater, your favorite restaurant, the park, the ice-cream parlor, whatever other places you go to. Assign a value to each property. As you decide whether Grandma's house is more valuable to your family than the movie, whether school is more important than church, and so forth, you will be making hard values decisions. Expect disagreement among family members, both in the naming of places and the assignment of values to them. The way your family works out your disagreements is a learning experience in itself.

Then it's time to make your "Chance" and "Community Chest" cards. More fun comes in as you write out cards that have special meaning. Some might say, "You forgot your Spanish homework, stay after school for three moves"; "You're finished with braces, take ten dollars to have dinner at your favorite restaurant"; "You broke a window in school, pay five weeks' allowance to the banker." To make the cards, all of you have to think about what would be good or bad for your family.

To play the game and bid for property, you all have to decide what you want to own the most and how much you're willing to pay for it—in other words, which places on your board carry the most meaning.

Strategy 51

SHOW AND TALK

Throughout her adult life, Eleanor Roosevelt was active in innumerable causes, many of which involved bettering the lives of children. It is probably significant that one of her earliest childhood memories was being taken by her father to the Thanksgiving dinner at a children's home called the Newsboys' Lodging House. Her uncle, Theodore Roosevelt, had become interested in the home as a result of having been taken there by *his* father.

Whenever we go out of our way to take our children places or to show them things, we are making impressions upon them. They will interpret our interests as things we value. What kinds of experiences do we want to share with our children? Which situations will we expose them to? Which people will we be sure to have them meet?

We can take our children to a commercial amusement park. We can wake them up in the middle of a summer night to bring sleeping bags out on the grass and watch the falling stars. We can take them to see Santa Claus to ask for Christmas presents. We can show them different neighborhoods. We can show them cultural treasures at an art museum, a concert, a library. We can expand their political awareness by taking them to a protest demonstration, to hear a candidate's speech, or to a session of the legislature. Whatever we go out of our way to show them says a lot about our values.

Besides the actual decisions that we make about taking our children places, we can deal with this issue through a multi-faceted Values Clarification strategy.

TIME: Any time.
PLACE: Anywhere you can write.
EQUIPMENT: Pencils and paper, kitchen timer.
PROCEDURE:

Part One: Parents list at least ten places, people, or events that their own parents took them to see as children. Check those items that you have taken your own children to see. Star those that made a lasting impression on you or influenced your life in some way. Take three minutes to recapture your memory of one of the starred items and tell how it has affected your life.

Part Two: Parents and children set priorities for the following groupings, by asking themselves, "As a parent, which would I most like to take my children to?"

a movie	an amusement park
a planetarium	a sauna at a friend's house
a class in woodworking	a tropical fish store
a fortune-teller	a horse race
a rock concert	a motorcycle show
a secondhand book store	bingo night at a church
the beach	the Salvation Army store
a baseball game	a big discount store
fishing	the most expensive furniture store in town

Examine your choices and see what patterns emerge. Which places have you actually gone to? Which have you all enjoyed the most? Which do you think you'd like to go to?

Part Three: Try these harder priorities:

a funeral   an X-rated film
your town's skid row   a porno book store
the emergency waiting   2 hours of TV soap opera
    room at a big city hospital

a home for retarded children
an old people's home
the waiting line at a state unemployment office

Use your priorities as the basis for family discussions, letting them lead toward the questions:

· What should parents show their children?
· What should children show their parents?
· How do people grow from experience?

Part Four: Everyone writes one "Ah-hah!" statement based on the above.

Strategy 52

WHAT'S IMPORTANT?

The following is the way the four members of one family expressed "Some of the Most Important Things We've Learned About Life":

· Sometimes, even when the consequences are bad, it is important to find out anyway.
· It's no use trying to figure out what happens when you die because you only get upset.
· You have to forget about what you've done and not say what you *should* have done.
· It's important to feel good about yourself before anything else.
· You have to be honest with people (including yourself).

- You can't always get what you want.
- You always need a good friend.
- The only way problems can be solved is by facing them, not running away.
- You should never expect too much from anything or anybody.
- Tell the truth (mostly).
- Try to know what you *really* want.
- You have to learn to live with yourself.
- You usually regret more what you didn't do than what you did do.
- Try to enjoy life in some way every day.
- You have to keep your sense of humor, no matter how bad things get.
- It's best to get your feelings out—even if it's icky and unpleasant at the time.
- You have to consider yourself and your own needs—and not worry too much about pleasing other people.
- You need goals to strive for.
- The key to happiness lies in how you feel about yourself.

Before we can live our life according to our values, we have to know which values are important to us. This strategy helps us find out.

TIME: Any time.
PLACE: Anywhere you can write.
EQUIPMENT: Paper and pencils, kitchen timer.
PROCEDURE: Everyone writes down "Five of the Most Important Things I've Learned About Life." For younger children, you could cut the number down to three, or even one. If you prefer, you could draw pictures to represent your "important things," instead of writing out the words.

Family members take turns reading their lists or explaining their drawings. You may need to remind everyone that no one's statements are to be laughed at or criticized. What is important for one person may not be so for another—but everyone's statement is right at that moment for that person.

After all have read their lists, each family member chooses one item to discuss. Each person elaborates for two or three minutes on why this aspect of life is important to him or her. Then other members respond, either affirming the importance of this principle to them or explaining—in a carefully worded, non-put-down fashion—why this principle is *not* important to them.

FOLLOW-UPS: Someone writes out a list of all the statements, or of one statement from each person, to display on the family bulletin board.

A few days later, ask, "Did we live any of these today?"

Ask everyone to read over the list to think whether there is anyone in his or her life who needs to know how he or she feels. How can you let those persons know of your feelings?

Through this strategy, the family sits down together, thinks about what every single member considers important, talks together, understands each other a little better, and perhaps comes a little closer to formulating guidelines for living a fulfilled life.

15

CLARIFYING RESPONSES

How do parents usually react when children tell about their thoughts, their feelings, or their conflicts? Sam says he got an "A" on a test, and his father says, "That's wonderful!" Terry admits she was sent to the principal because she has been late for school five times in the past two weeks, and her mother says, "I told you to leave the house earlier." Victor tells that his (erstwhile) best friend socked him in the jaw, and his parents say, "That's some good friend. You ought to get rid of him."

These reactions are typical. But they are not helpful. Children don't need our judgments, and they don't always need our advice. On an emotional level they need our sympathetic understanding. On an intellectual level they need our help in relating their feelings and actions in the most effective way. We can help them with Clarifying Responses.

Clarifying responses are brief questions that respond to children's own statements and stimulate them to put everyday feelings and events into a larger framework. They make it easier for children to look at their opinions, beliefs, and actions and to make up their own minds. The right question may make one child realize she has options she had not thought about before. It can make another consider whether his plan is really the best course of action. When children have problems to resolve, conflicts to settle or decisions to make, they are *not* helped by our telling them what to do. They *are* helped by our raising questions that help them make up their own minds.

Clarifying responses need not lead to a long discussion. They are usually most effective when they do nothing more than raise a question. Most exchanges involving clarifying responses can be considered "one-legged talks" because they are so brief they can be completed while standing on one leg.

For example, 11-year-old Rosa came home from school one day and told her mother, "I wish Miss Dirksen would stop telling us how great the other soccer teams are. Every time we have a game she says, 'You've gotta work hard today, girls. That's a tough team you're playing against.' Then we get so nervous we can hardly play."

Mother asks, "Is there anything you could do about that?"

"I guess I could say something to her," says Rosa, "but *I* can't tell a grownup what to do."

Mother helps Rosa get in touch with her feelings by asking, "Does what she's saying now really matter a lot to you?"

"Well," says Rosa, "the way it is now, I hate the games."

At this point the "one-legged talk" could end, with Rosa continuing to mull over her problem, unpressured to come to an immediate solution but aware that she can bring the issue up again.

Not every question needs an immediate answer. Often it is more helpful to pose more questions. This way, Rosa—or any child—can consider more facets of the problem. She is likely to think about it on her own, and she may come back to discuss it further. Or she may make her decision without further discussion.

Not every problem can be solved with a clarifying response or two. Emotional problems do not always lend themselves to this brief, open-ended approach. More complex issues require more extensive discussion. Even in these instances, though, communication is often easier when parents gently prod with clarifying responses, instead of coming on strong with advice or judgments.

The essence of Values Clarification is the need for each person to work out his or her own right answers. To ward off the temptation to preach or moralize, it is best—at the beginning, anyway —to stay away from the clarifying responses in situations you disapprove of. Knowing your feelings, your child will sense a rebuke in your questions, and from that time on, the questions themselves may come across as critical. If you get started on less controversial, less emotional issues, clarifying responses will gradually become a way of life. They will serve as one more tool you can use to help your children deal with the many issues they will have to act upon in their lives.

A list of sample clarifying responses appears below. Read through them and familiarize yourself with the general approach. Phrase your questions in your own words, though. Clarifying responses can help your children consider what choices are open, think about the consequences of each one, analyze their feelings about the issues, and explore actions that would be satisfying.

SOME CLARIFYING RESPONSES:

· Is this something that you ⎰ prize?
feel good about?
are proud of?
like to do?

· Is this something that is important in your life?
· Are you glad about that?
· How do you feel about that?

· How did you feel when ⎰ that happened?
she/he said that?
she/he did that?
you said/did that?

· Have you felt this way for a long time?
· Was that your idea?

· Was that something that you yourself ⎰ selected?
chose?
decided?

· Did you consider any other ways of acting?
· Was there anything else you could have said/done?
· Could there have been any other way of handling that situation?

- Was that a free choice of yours—or did you feel you *had* to do it?
- Did anybody put any pressure on you to do that?
- Do you do anything about that idea?
- Do you do this often?
- Would you like to do it more often?
- Is there any reason why you can't do it more often?
- Is there anything you can do about that?
- Can you give me some examples of what you mean?
- What do you mean by . . . ?
- Can you define that word?
- What does that word/idea mean to you?
- Where would that notion lead to?
- What would be the consequence of that?
- What do you think would happen if you did that?
- Would you really *do* that—or is it just something you like to think about?
- Are you saying that . . . ? (repeat what child has just said)
- Did you say that . . . ? (repeat in some distorted way, hoping that the child will correct your distortion)
- Have you thought much about that idea/behavior/action?
- What are some good things about that idea/plan/situation?
- What would have to happen for things to work out that way?
- Is there anything you could do to make that happen?
- Is what you say/do about this consistent with . . . ? (point out something that had been said about something else)
- What other possibilities are there?
- What else could you do?
- Is that your own personal preference, or do you think most people should believe/do that?
- How can I help you do something about your idea?
- Is there anyone who could help you do something about that?
- Do you have a plan/purpose in back of this activity?
- Is that very important to you?

- Would you like to tell others about $\begin{cases} \text{the way you think?} \\ \text{what you do?} \end{cases}$

- Do you have any special reasons for saying/doing that?
- Would you do the same thing over again?
- What do you think you might do differently?
- How do you know that is right?
- Do you value that?
- Do you think that is important in your life?
- Do you think you will always believe that?
- In what way would your life be different without this?
- Would this be a better world if more people did that?

16

DECISIONS, DECISIONS

Beth wants to be a Brownie Scout, and she wants to try out for the school swimming team. Both meet Wednesday afternoons. Calvin had been looking forward to going to camp this summer, but he has been offered a job helping out at his uncle's gas station. Denise wants to enter an art competition, but has to work on a social studies report due the same week. Eli had promised to help Farrell, his best friend, study for a math test, and then Hank invited him to a World Series game for the same day. Gerry is supposed to pitch for her baseball team in a crucial game, but her parents want her to attend her grandfather's 75th birthday party.

Children are constantly faced with decisions. While some of them may seem trivial to adults, all are important to the children. The way they learn to make decisions sets a pattern that will be continued throughout their lives. These decisions often involve such conflicting values as service to others versus physical fitness, friendship versus a love of baseball, and meeting family expectations versus meeting teammates' expectations.

Such values-conflicting decisions are not easy. The more tools we give our children, the better equipped they will be to evaluate the implications of their decisions. Too often the temptation for parents is to say, "I know what's best for my child."

But this approach has two problems. First, even assuming that we are right, our telling our children what to do won't teach them anything about decision-making. Secondly, we are *not* always right. We sometimes regret our own decisions and feel we might have been wiser to have done something else. How, then, can we presume to say that we always know what our children should do? In his bold book *Escape from Childhood,* John Holt says,

> . . . on the whole, most of the time, every human being knows better than anyone else what he needs and wants, what gives him pleasure and joy or causes suffering and pain. Given real choices, people will choose for themselves better than others will choose for them.

We have to let our children learn how to make decisions and deal with the consequences. Maybe, for example, Denise's career in art could be launched through this competition. Maybe Eli would be so resentful because he passed up the ball game to help Farrell that their friendship might be irreparably damaged. Maybe the camp experience might be more valuable than the money Calvin could earn. We don't have all the answers; we must let our children search for theirs themselves.

Decisions are not always an either/or proposition. Often there are more than two alternatives. There may be a wide range of choices besides the two that first come to mind. Maybe Calvin can work part of the summer and go to camp for part, or maybe he can earn money at camp. Maybe Denise can prevail upon her social studies teacher to grant her an extension on her report, or maybe she can tie in her artwork to a social studies theme—and fulfill both goals at once. Maybe Eli can help Farrell and get to the ball game a little late.

A child learns more by making the wrong decision by himself than by making the right one because we told him to. We learn more from our own mistakes than from other people's correct actions. If Calvin passes up the job at his uncle's gas station and then finds that he doesn't have the money to buy the ten-speed bike he wants; if Denise ignores her social studies report and fails the course; if Eli loses a valued friendship because he went to the ball game—then these children will be learning far more than they could ever learn from all our advice and admonitions.

Clarifying responses provide one tool for helping children make up their minds. But sometimes it helps to formalize the decision-making process even more. Many of us are familiar with the old Ben Franklin way of making up our minds—writing down all the factors in favor of a decision on one side and all those against it on the other side—and then weighing the lists of pros and cons. This method is fine as far as it goes, but it does not always go far enough.

The Clarifying Grid (see pages 166–67), built on the Seven Steps to Values, allows for a diversity of choices. In any particular situation you may think of questions not on this grid. This is meant only as a model—as a launching pad from which you can develop your own.

Step 1: Option Exploration, calls for brainstorming to explore possible alternatives. List *all* the things you *could* do, even if some of them seem crazy. Sometimes an idea that seems harebrained at first will turn out to be the best solution. And sometimes an outlandish notion will spark your imagination toward some more realistic solution. So don't be afraid to fly. This first row embodies the search for alternatives that is a basic element of Values Clarification. It also implies the notion of compromise.

Many of our actions are based on compromises between what we want to do in two different areas. We may not be able to have our cake and eat it, too. But we can compromise. We can eat half the cake—and keep the other half. We can bake two cakes. We can eat something else. We can keep looking for compromises we can live with.

Compromise is sometimes thought of as a "dirty" word, because it is often used in the sense of betraying our values. But very often we have two conflicting, equally valid sets of values. The only way to satisfy them both is to make some sort of compromise. Wars are averted through compromise. Marriages are enriched through compromise. Life without compromise is inconceivable.

Step 2: Consequence Count, leads us to consider the consequences of our choices. At this point some options will be eliminated because of totally unacceptable consequences.

Often we don't know what the consequences of a course of action will be. We need more information before we can make a free and intelligent choice.

Step 3: Free Choice, provides places for us to enter the information we need and the people who could give us the information and advice that would help us to understand better what our choice would involve.

In *Step 4: Accent on the Positive,* we think about how we would feel about the consequences, and we rank them in order, from most to least desirable.

Step 5: Rooftop Shout, brings up the question, Is this something we would be proud and happy to have the whole world know about? (If the action is one we would prefer to keep private, why is that? And would we want to do it, anyway?)

Step 6: Values Action, spurs us to consider the first thing we can do to carry out our decision, and *Step 7: Pattern-Building,* encourages us to think how we can fit it into our lives on an ongoing basis.

Let's see how the grid works. Francisco, 10, is on a neighborhood baseball team. Lately he has been unhappy because his coach doesn't put him into play as often as he would like. Francisco is on the third string of the team. "I know I'm not as good as some of those other guys," he says, "but still it's not fair. If Coach never lets me play, I'll *never* get as good as them. And it seems like a big waste of time for me to keep going out for practice and to go to all the games—and then to have to sit on the bench for most of the time. It's a waste of money for the uniform, too. And I feel so stupid. I oughta get off the team!"

What should Francisco do? How can his parents help him? The filled-out grid represents the culmination of a decision-making session when both his parents sat down with Francisco to help him explore his options. By the time Francisco got to Step 4, he had decided that what he most wanted was special coaching that might help him become a better player.

By Step 6, Francisco had decided to ask around school in a roundabout way to try to find out whether any of the other youngsters had ever had coaching and who had given it. Mean-

THE CLARIFYING GRID

	STAY ON TEAM	GIVE UP BASEBALL
1. *Option Exploration:* What are all the different things I could do about this?		
2. *Consequence Count:* What are the probable consequences of each course of action?	*stay with friends keep getting frustrated hate coach sit out a lot	not see my friends be bored feel like failure let my parents down not play at all
—What consequences can I absolutely not accept?		don't want to
3. *Free Choice:* What do I need to find out to give me enough information to choose freely?	Will coach ever let me play more?	
—Who can help me?	Coach	
4. *Accent on the Positive:* Star the consequences I would feel good about. Rank them in order from most to least desirable.		
5. *Rooftop Shout:* Check those I'd want the world to know about.		
6. *Values Action:* What is the first thing I should do to carry out my decision?		
7. *Pattern-Building:* What can I do on a regular basis to support my decision?		

166

LOOK FOR LESS COMPETITIVE TEAM	TAKE LESSONS AND PRACTICE	GET A NEW COACH
have to get in with new kids _____ *play more _____ might not like it might be hard to get to	give up time _____ *play better *surprise everybody embarrassed if friends found out _____ homework would suffer	*like game more *probably play more old coach would be mad at me _____ so would his son, my friend
		too hard
Where is one? Who's on it? How would I get to it?	Who could teach me? Where? When? How many would I need? How much would it cost? Could we afford it?	
Gym teacher Little League office "Y"	Gym teacher Other kids who took lessons Little League office "Y" Parents	
	Francisco: ask kids if they know someone _____ *Father:* call "Y" & Little League _____ *Mother:* call other parents	
	Work out a schedule for practice	

while, his father offered to try to find a coach by calling the "Y" and the local Little League office, and his mother agreed to telephone some parents of young ballplayers. If the coaching turned out not to work out well, or if no coach could be found, the family could get together again. The next step might be to look for a less competitive team.

This approach has several pluses. The decision is essentially Francisco's. His parents force themselves to remember that and not to impose their own ideas about what he should do. But the boy is not left alone with his decision. He is helped to look at all the ramifications. Furthermore, formalizing the decision through the grid provides a structure that Francisco may remember the next time he faces a dilemma. Finally, this method tries to uncover and utilize all relevant information that could help the boy make up his mind.

One mother who encouraged her children to use the clarifying grid was delighted to hear 11-year-old Cathy grumble, "Now it seems like I have to make all my decisions myself anymore."

PART TWO

17

ISSUES THAT COUNT

"Why is it so hard for some children to keep friends?"

"How much television should a child watch?"

"What should a child's allowance cover?"

These are a few of the countless values-related questions that crop up in every family. Values Clarification can make the answers easier to find. The concept of Values Clarification goes far beyond games played at the family dinner table. It reaches into the farthest corners of our lives, affecting our beliefs and actions about every issue that touches us.

Sometimes it is more apropos to think about values in terms of a particular question, or issue, instead of starting out with a strategy. Most of the issues that concern us fit into the Ten Values-rich Areas: Family, Self, Friendship, Society, Morals and Ethics, Religion, Leisure, Money, Work and School, and Love and Sexuality.

You have learned the basic approach of Values Clarification, and you have worked with some or all of the basic fifty-two strategies. You now have all the tools you need to tackle any issue. This chapter and those that follow give suggestions for making up new strategies or adapting old ones to deal with those topics most likely to come up in family life.

SOME WAYS TO DISCUSS ASPECTS OF THE TEN VALUES-RICH AREAS:

Ask everyone in the family to rank these ten areas in the order of their importance. This is difficult since all of the areas are abstract and complex. But forcing yourselves to rank them gets you all thinking about the relative values you place on different facets of your lives.

To make it easier for everyone to re-examine these rankings, pose questions that involve conflicts, such as:

· If your family were going away for a weekend and you had the chance to go someplace more exciting with a friend, with whom would you go? (Friendship vs. Family)
· What would your decision be if both trips were to last a week? (Friendship vs. Family)
· Would you spend your own money to go with a friend to a movie that you didn't particularly want to see, or would you save your money by letting your friend go without you? (Friendship vs. Money)
· Would you take a job you don't like that pays well? (Work vs. Money)
· Would you cheat on an exam to get into medical school? (Morals and Ethics vs. Work)
· Would you drive yourself so hard at work that you wouldn't have any time to relax so you could relax later on in life? (Money vs. Leisure)
· Would you give up a party you really want to go to to go out with your parents on their aniversary? (Family vs. Self)
· Would you join an organization that favors legalized abortion because you feel that's better for society, even though your religion forbids it? (Society vs. Religion)

Pick one of the ten areas as the focus for a strategy you are already familiar with. For example, here are some ways that Strategy 1, My Favorite Things, can be adapted to the values-rich areas:

Ask people to list "Twenty Things I Love to Do . . ."

· with a special friend
· with someone I love
· with my family

· in my leisure time
· that don't cost any money
· that are related to work or school
· that are related to my religion

Or ask them to think of "Twenty Things I Could Do . . ."

· for the cause of ecology, peace, relations between the races, or some other societal issue
· for my own health and safety

The following strategies are also especially adaptable to a wide range of issues:

2:	Ah-hah!	13: Lucky Thirteen
3:	The Whip	16: Are You Someone Who
5:	Priorities	. . .?
6:	Values Spectrum	42: Family Interview
7:	Family Voting	48: Drawing the Line
8:	Provocative Questions	49: Family Bulletin Board

Pick an area that is currently a source of conflict or confusion within your family and make up a strategy (or apply one from this book) on that topic. If, for example, your child has trouble making friends, you might rank in order the qualities that make a good friend. Or if your child does not want to go to Sunday School, you might base a Values Spectrum on religious observance.

In these discussions, though, do not try to manipulate your children toward a predetermined conclusion. The discussions should be vehicles through which you and your children can clarify your thinking, not vehicles to propel your children toward the destination you have in mind. The minute this aim is subverted by moralizing, the effectiveness of the approach dissolves.

The following ten chapters carry many suggestions for exploring each of the Ten Values-rich Areas. They will help you to start to build your own values discussions in ways and on issues that are most relevant to your own family.

18

FAMILY STRATEGIES

The honesty and positive emphasis of Values Clarification can help family members grow closer. Here are some strategies built around the concept of family.

The Here and Now Wheel (Strategy 18): This is especially useful during times of conflict—between brother and sister, parent and child, or husband and wife. When tempers flare and feelings are hurt, the wheel helps people get in touch with their own feelings and to share those feelings directly and honestly with the people they need to share them with.

I Wonder . . . (Strategy 3): This works as a whip, with everyone in the family asked to complete the sentence. People say things like, "I wonder when you will realize that I have to make certain decisions for myself." "I wonder why we're having so much trouble talking to each other these days." "I wonder how we can show our love for each other more." This is most effective when it builds on a discussion about an issue that really matters to the family, and it can often keep communication on a positive note when dealing with sensitive areas.

What Is One Area Where I Feel My Parents/Children Don't Understand Me? Everyone writes out his or her answer to this question. Other family members try to guess what everyone wrote. Afterward, people share their answers and talk about the gaps between what they wrote and what the others guessed. End with "I wonder . . ." statements.

A Moment of Closeness: Everyone thinks of one instance when she or he felt special closeness to a parent, child, or sibling. Everyone speaks for two minutes about what happened and what the feelings were.

Family Moments to Remember (Strategy 22): The starter asks everyone to think of one special memory in one category such as the ones listed below. Everyone answers, "whip"-style. Afterward, people are asked, "Which of these do we want to have happen again?" and "How can we make plans to be sure that it will happen again?"
Some kinds of pleasant memories:

· on a picnic
· at a fair
· when Grandma or Grandpa came
· making music
· dancing
· playing games
· in the snow
· on a boat
· on an airplane
· in a restaurant
· at a party
· at bedtime

Validating Notes: How would you feel if you reached into your coat pocket and pulled out a note that said, "Dear Mommy, You made me so happy when you didn't holler at me last night even though my friends made such a mess in the playroom. Thank you for understanding. Love, Benji."

A few moments taken here or there to write a brief note, which can be tucked into a pocket, a lunchbox, a handbag, or somewhere else where the recipient will come upon it unexpectedly can make for bright moments in a day. Without requiring notes on any set schedule, the family that gets into the habit of writing them to each other is building good feelings that are bound to be treasured.

High Points Chart: Once a week everyone writes down the high point of being a parent or a child for that week. The chart is posted on the family bulletin board.

High Points Calendar: The weekly high points are written on the calendar and saved so that the family can look back in years to come to recapture these delicious high points.

Priorities (Strategy 5): Your mother and father fight all the time. What seems to you like the best solution to their problems?

- get a divorce
- see a marriage counselor
- try to gloss over their differences until the kids grow up

Rank in order what you think would be the ideal family size for you as an adult:

- 4 or more children
- 3 children
- 2 children
- 1 child
- no children

Why do you feel the way you do?
What would you do if the person you marry feels differently?
Rank in order the most important reasons why you would want to have children:

- someone to care for you in your old age
- bring husband and wife closer together
- fulfill a woman/prove manhood
- carry on the race
- children are fun

- duty to society (intelligent people have obligation to bring more of own kind into world)
- give your parents grandchildren
- carry on the family name
- have someone to love
- other

Family Rituals and Holidays: On Christmas day in the Simon home, the youngest child goes to the tree to get the presents he has made. As he gives them, one by one, to each member of the family, he tells how he came to make each gift and what it means to him. Everyone else in the family follows this routine, and what with meals and other activities, the last gifts are not given out until after dinner.

Sam Wendkos could always find his children in a crowd because of the special whistle he made up, which the children learned and taught to their children.

Whenever the five members of the Leaf family are all around the dinner table after not having eaten together for several days, they do a "Family Circle." Everyone crosses arms and holds hands with his or her neighbor. One person makes a wish, then squeezes the hand of the person on his or her right; that person then makes a wish and squeezes, and so on. When the last person has wished, the squeeze goes back in the other direction.

A family's rituals bind its members together in a very special way. This strategy can help you appreciate some of the special things you do together:

Write down five rituals that your family observes. They can be small or large, based on holidays or birthdays, or part of everyday life. Share your lists, and each talk for one minute about one special ritual; tell why it is especially important to you or describe one special time.

So often we continue to celebrate holidays the way we always have, without considering how we could enrich their meaning. When we think carefully about them, the whole family benefits. For example, your children have some sixty to seventy Thanksgiving dinners ahead of them. If you encourage them to think about the significance of the holiday, their Thanksgivings will become more meaningful with every year. Here are two strategies for Thanksgiving:

Thanksgiving Priorities:
Which of these would be the worst kind of Thanksgiving Day?

· if you had to work all day in the pickle factory
· if you sent out for a pizza for Thanksgiving dinner
· if Mother spent two days cooking a big turkey dinner with your favorite pumpkin pie—and the family ate it in 12½ minutes and then all rushed out to watch a football game leaving Mother with the dirty dishes

Thanksgiving Whip: Everyone at the dinner table says one thing that she or he is thankful for.

Gift-giving is an area fraught with values. The following two strategies are especially meaningful around the Christmas-Chanukah season.

The Last Gift: Write down the last gift you gave every family member. Code the list:

U the person could really use it
Y you liked it yourself
W you wanted the person to have it for special reasons
P you thought the person would want it

Think about the recipients' reactions to your gifts. Did they reflect your feelings in giving them?

If you gave someone a gift she or he didn't like, which would you most want the recipient to do? Rank in order the following:

· pretend to like it
· tell you they were exchanging it for something they really wanted
· exchange it without telling you
· give it to someone else who really did like it

The holidays are filled with values issues. Can you adapt strategies or make up new ones to help you decide, for example, whom to send greeting cards to or how to make your holiday letters more meaningful?

Birthdays are also special occasions that can be enhanced with the Values Clarification approach, as, for example, in the following three strategies:

Birthday Dreams Can Come True (Strategy 10): All family members get two minutes to describe the ideal way they would celebrate their next birthday. They are encouraged to describe it from morning to night—what they'd eat at every meal, what they'd do, and whom they would be with. The rest of the family listens closely, and when the time comes, they try to make the real birthday come as close as possible to the ideal.

Birthday Validations: Instead of sending each other cards, try one of these. The whole family can get together to make a validation collage, a collection of lovely pictures and cartoons and sentences showing how everyone appreciates the birthday person. Or family members might draw up lists of special things for which they want to validate the birthday celebrant. The list might number as many validations as there are years in his or her age.

Strategies Go to the Party: At Julie Stenger's seventh birthday party, she and her friends sat on the front lawn and did "I Wonders," "Magic Box" (using a toy chest), and "Dreams Can Come True".

As you can see, the possibility for adapting strategies to family issues is limited only by your own imagination. The more you bring Values Clarification into your daily life, the more you will get out of it.

19

STRATEGIES ABOUT THE SELF

Many of us have been brought up to feel as if thinking about ourselves and what we want out of life is egotistical and selfish. And yet most of us do think about ourselves a great deal of the time. These strategies help us think constructively about ourselves—our personalities, our health and safety, our sex roles— so we can lead more fulfilling lives.

Priorities (Strategy 5):
Which would you most like to improve about yourself?

- your looks
- your personality
- your brainpower
- your athletic ability

Would you rather be thought of as:

- creative
- funny
- smart?

Which of these would you like to gct better at?

- boldly ask for affection
- show your emotions more easily
- stop making self-put-downs

Which of these three risks is the most stupid to take?

- to start smoking cigarettes as a teenager
- to ride a bicycle after dark without lights
- to play "chicken" on the railroad tracks

Which drug is the most harmful?

- alcohol
- tobacco
- marijuana
- caffeine
- LSD

Which do you think is the worst problem for a teenager?

- to become (or get someone) pregnant without being married
- to be dependent upon hard drugs
- to drop out of school
- to have a boyfriend or girlfriend of another race
- to be arrested

You don't feel like having a drink. What would you be most likely to do if you're at a party where everyone's urging you to drink?

- take one drink, sip it slowly, and eat a lot
- say you're in training, you're on a diet, you're allergic to alcohol, or some other fib
- take a drink and later pour it out
- say you don't drink and give no explanation
- say you don't want a drink and give your reasons

Values Spectrum (Strategy 6):

TEETOTALER TERESA . . .	DRINKING DORIS
believes no one of any age should ever drink any alcohol because it's the devil's potion.	loves to drink herself and gives her 5-year-old child a drink every day so she'll learn how to handle alcohol.

IT'LL HEAL IKE . . . . .
won't use a bandage on a cut, and drags his broken leg behind him, splintless.

DOCTORING DUDLEY
calls the doctor three times a day, after taking his own blood pressure.

BLIND BERTHA . . . . .
never looks at any label—gargles with household cleaning fluids, uses battery acid for salad dressings.

CAUTIOUS CAROLYN
goes into restaurant kitchens to read labels on their containers because she won't eat any drop of food unless she knows every single ingredient in it.

Food Diary: This is especially good if any member of the family needs to lose weight or eat special foods. Everyone writes down everything eaten for a week and codes the foods as follows:

* high in nutritional value
X junk food, low in nutrients
+ high in calories
− low in calories
F high in saturated fats
2 this would not have been on your list two years ago
S snack
M mealtime
H home
A away

Write an "Ah-hah!" statement (Strategy 2) about what you have learned about your eating habits.

Write a statement that begins, "I resolve . . ." if you want to make any changes about your eating habits.

Safety Forced-Choice Ladder Game: This game has two parts, one for adults, which the children administer, and one for children, which the adults administer. Everyone gets a big piece of paper and is asked to draw a ladder with eight rungs. The starter reads out the following items and tells people to write the key word for each item on the ladder, according to its importance. The most important items would be on the top rung, the least important on the bottom. Here are the ladder items:

For Children:

1. Never taking candy from a stranger (Key Word: candy)
2. Always attaching a safety flag to your bike (flag)
3. Never bicycling at night without a light (light)
4. Wearing a helmet on a mini-bike or when jumping a regular bike (helmet)
5. Double-knotting your shoelaces so you don't trip (laces)
6. Never taking pills that you don't know everything about (pills)
7. Always wearing seat belts in a car (seat belts)
8. Crossing streets only at the corners (corners)
9. Not running with a popsicle or lollipop in your mouth (running)
10. Never playing with plastic bags (plastic)
11. Staying away from abandoned refrigerators and freezers (fridge)
12. Reporting any puncture wounds and getting a tetanus shot (puncture)

For Adults:

1. Always using a grounding plug adapter on a drill (adapter)
2. Never mowing the lawn barefoot or in flimsy shoes (mowing)
3. Always using the emergency brake when parking a car (brake)
4. Always wearing seat belts in a car (seat belts)
5. Avoiding more than five cups of coffee a day (coffee)
6. Putting non-skid strips in the bathtub (skid)
7. Wearing white at night when walking on country roads (road)

8. Stopping at railroad crossings when the red lights are on (RR)
9. Keeping your weight down (fat)
10. Putting up a no-smoking sign in your house (smoking)
11. Installing a fire extinguisher near the kitchen stove (fire)
12. Fixing a tire that is wearing thin (tire)

Family Voting about Male/Female Roles (Strategy 7): How many of you . . .

1. think girls should know how to change tires on a car?
2. think boys should learn how to cook?
3. think that fathers should have as much responsibility as mothers for raising children?
4. think children whose mothers work have more problems than children whose mothers stay home?
5. ever cry in the movies?
6. think any woman who wants an abortion should be allowed to get one?
7. would choose to have a son if you were only going to have one child?
8. think women should keep their maiden names after they get married?
9. think women are more emotional than men?
10. think men are naturally more mechanical?

My Favorite Things (Strategy 1): Write down "Ten Things I Love to Do." Make another list of "Ten Things I Would Love to Do If I Were of the Opposite Sex." Compare the two lists. Are they different? Why or why not?

Presents: Children, write down the last five presents you bought for your friends' birthdays. Adults, write down the last five presents you bought for your children. Go back over the list and check the ones you would still have bought if the recipient were of the opposite sex. If there are differences, why? Share and discuss your lists.

Growing Old: Write down ten things you did today that gave you pleasure. Circle the ones you will still be able to do when you are past 65. Write and share "Ah-hah!" statements. To follow up: Make a list of ten things you regularly enjoy doing that you will *not* be able to do when you are 65. For each one of these, think of something equally pleasant that you will be able to do at that age. Discuss the implications for your life today.

20

FRIENDSHIP STRATEGIES

The genuine friendship of people who care for us, who want to be in our company, and who desire our happiness and welfare is one of the sweetest gifts of life. Children are particularly friend-conscious. They want to be with their friends, and they want to know that their friends make efforts to be with them. They become uneasy when they sense the dissolution of a friendship, even if the lack of interest is on their own part.

Here are some strategies and questions to spur a family's thinking about friends and friendship and to provide the kind of reflecting that nourishes special relationships.

Lucky Thirteen (Strategy 13): List thirteen friends you like to see. Cross out the three you'd leave off your list if you were having a party restricted to only ten persons. Circle the three names you'd invite if you could ask only three. Write one word by each of these three names describing what gift of self they give to you or you to them. Pick one of the three and talk for two minutes about why you like this person so much.

My Favorite Things (Strategy 1): Think of a particular friend. Write down Twenty Things You Love to Do with This Friend. Or code your list of favorite things, indicating which items you think would be on your special friend's list.

Priorities (Strategy 5): If your best friend had an unpleasant body odor, what would you be most likely to do?

186

- buy him or her a deodorant
- tell him/her, "You ought to take a bath more often."
- write an anonymous note
- stop seeing the friend
- nothing

Values Spectrum (Strategy 6): Everyone places him/herself somewhere between these extremes:

LONE WOLF	PACK WOLF
You like your own company better than anyone else's. You like to be alone so much you give a birthday party for yourself, and you're the only guest.	You hate to be alone. You want other people around you all the time, even when you go to sleep, take a shower, or write in your diary.

Quadrant of Opposites: Everyone divides a sheet of paper into four quadrants. In the upper left, family members list ten people with whom they like to spend time. In the upper right, they list ten places they like to go and feel happy when they are there. In the lower left section, they list five people with whom they *don't* like to spend time. In the lower right, they list five places that make them unhappy, where they don't like to spend much time.

Let's look at this information on opposites with the tools of Values Clarification. What do we learn when we ask questions like these:

- How often have you taken the people you like to be with to the places where you like to be?
- What would happen if you took the ten people you like to be with, one at a time, to the five places where you don't like to spend time?
- Would it ruin the places you like if you took the people you don't like to be with to those places?
- Do you think there's any chance that any of the people in the lower left-hand quadrant might ever belong in the upper left-hand quadrant? What would have to happen?
- How are the people in the two quadrants different?

Finish up the strategy by sharing "Ah-hah!" statements.

The Ideal Friend: Everyone lists ten characteristics an ideal friend should have. Code your lists, thinking of your two or three best friends, and putting their initials next to those traits that you think they have.

Then ask some questions, like: If your friends don't have many of the ideal characteristics, why are they your friends? What other strengths do they have?

Ralph Waldo Emerson once said, "The only way to have a friend is to be one." Examine yourself with regard to the ten ideal traits. Code your list with a star next to all the traits you feel *you* possess. Is there one in particular that you would like to work on developing? Can you think of one concrete act you could perform that would help strengthen that trait? Do you want to make a self-contract to do it? (See Strategy 28: Contract with Yourself.)

21

SOCIETY STRATEGIES

The values we hold as individuals determine the way we will build our society—how its laws will be written and enforced, how its institutions will be structured and administered, the quality of life for all its citizens. Not until we as individuals have thought through major issues can we try to fulfill our civic responsibilities.

What are our responsibilities, as individuals, to society in general? Psychiatrist Karl Menninger puts it this way: "If a dozen people are in a lifeboat, and one of them discovers a leak near where he is sitting, is there any doubt as to his responsibility? Not for having made the hole, or for finding it, but for attempting to repair it. To ignore it or to keep silent about it is almost equivalent to having made it."

Values Clarification can help us and our families find the leaks in society—and then find ways to repair them. This chapter offers suggestions for using the strategies to deal with such major issues as peace, the environment, the rights of all people for equal opportunity, and our political system.

Our children will be reaching voting age sooner than we realize. The more they have thought about political issues, the more they will be able to contribute to society.

Family Voting (Strategy 7) is a good springboard for political discussion. The starter can say, "I want to ask you a few questions about this whole business of elections just so we can see where some of our values are. There are no right answers to any of them, and we should have some fun seeing where we all stand. Whenever anyone else feels like it—tomorrow night, maybe, or next week—you can bring in some questions to the dinner table and we'll vote on your questions, too. (See page 61 for directions on Family Voting.)

Here are ten questions related to voting:

1. How many here have ever been inside a voting booth?
2. How many think that parents should take pre-schoolers into the voting booth with them, to give them some awareness of the election process?
3. How many think it is a waste of your vote to cast a ballot for a candidate who has no hope of winning? And that it would be better to vote for the lesser of two evils?
4. How many think that casting a vote for a candidate who expresses your views exactly but has no chance of winning is a good way to show the other candidates how you feel?
5. How many have ever worn a button supporting a political candidate?
6. How many have ever passed out political literature?
7. How many would ever ring doorbells trying to get support for a candidate?
8. How many would give up a week's allowance to support a candidate?
9. How many would tear down signs of a rival candidate?
10. Do you think children of any age should be permitted to vote?

After the voting, pick up on those questions that seem to have the most possibilities for further talk. Keep the conversation on a level everyone can understand. Don't get on a soapbox. Feel free to express your own opinions (ideally, after the children have expressed theirs), but resist the temptation to proselytize.

Let the conversation run its natural course, and if it meanders to ball scores or TV shows, that's okay, too. Just by raising issues, you will have gotten people to think about them in a new way.

Priorities (Strategy 5):
Which of these do you think is most important for the next President to deal with?

· keeping our country at peace
· keeping prices at a level most people can afford
· preserving our environment

If a family with the same number, sexes, and ages of children as yours were to move next door, rank in order which of these families you would most want as new neighbors:

· one of a different race
· one from a different country, none of whom speak English
· one who practices a different religion
· a family of your race and religion and nationality

Which of these would be the hardest to talk to your parents about?

· having a boyfriend or girl friend of a different race
· your desire to attend church with a friend of a different religion
· your plans to adopt interracially instead of having children of your own

How do you think a country should keep itself strong?

· Offer good money and good training so people will volunteer to serve in a standing army.
· Draft all young men and women to serve their country for two years, either in the army or in other service jobs.
· Forget about keeping any army and concentrate on getting rid of poverty around the world and building up a strong diplomatic corps.

Imagine that you are a slave whose master has just threatened to give you a brutal whipping because of some infraction of his rules. After thinking about the consequences, rank in order which of the following you decide to do:

- run away
- fight the master
- take the whipping

Unfair Treatment: "How do you respond when you think you are being treated unfairly?" All family members tell the story behind the most recent time they had this feeling—what happened, how they felt, and what they did. Looking back, ask yourselves whether there was anything else you could have done.

What One Person Can Do: Everyone makes a list of "Ten Things I Could Do for the Environment." Each person then checks off the items that she or he actually does do. People share their lists. As a final step, each person decides to do one additional thing and to incorporate that into his or her regular lifestyle.

Family Diplomacy: Everyone thinks of three situations when your family negotiated a difference of opinion and reached a solution everyone could accept. What similarities are there between what you did and what nations do in the UN?

22

MORALS AND ETHICS STRATEGIES

Are you trustworthy, loyal, helpful, friendly, courteous, kind, obedient, cheerful, thrifty, brave, clean, and reverent? When we talk about morals and ethical behavior, we often talk in terms of the Boy Scout law. But what do these words mean when they are translated into action? Are they absolutes, to be followed at all times? How can we break down these abstract words into concepts and situations and decisions that are meaningful for our own values systems, and for the way we lead our lives?

OBEDIENCE

From our earliest years we are taught to obey—first parents, then teachers, then employers, superiors in the armed forces, governmental officials—anyone duly constituted as a person in authority. Most people feel uncomfortable *not* obeying the orders of someone they perceive as an authority, even when such disobedience is in their own best interests or in accord with the dictates of their own conscience.

Psychologist Stanley Milgram carried out experiments at Yale University to test the amount of pain one ordinary person would inflict upon another, just because he was ordered to do so by an experimenter. His horrifying findings were that in all repetitions of the experiment, most persons were willing to administer electric shocks that they thought were extremely painful and possibly dangerous. (In reality, they were neither. The anguished "victims" were, unbeknownst to the subjects of the experiment, actors pretending to feel the pain.) Many of the subjects in this experiment were very uncomfortable with their role in inflicting pain—*but they did it anyway.* They excused themselves from responsibility for their actions by their sense of duty to the experiment itself and by the fact that they were just following someone else's orders.

This experiment illustrates a classic values conflict, put this way by one of the subjects after he had learned the real purpose of the experiment:

> What appalled me was that I could possess this capacity for obedience and compliance to a central idea., i.e., the value of a memory experiment, even after it became clear that continued obedience to this value was at the expense of violation of another value., i.e., don't hurt someone who is helpless and not hurting you. . . . I hope I deal more effectively with any future conflicts of values I encounter.*

Families can discuss the Milgram experiments and also ask themselves these provocative questions:

· Can you think of a time when you experienced conflict between obedience and some other value? What happened? What did you do and how did you feel about it? What do you think you would do in a similar situation today?
· Do you think that children should *always* obey their parents? If not, when should they? Does the age of the child matter? Are there any circumstances under which complete obedience is necessary?
· What criteria can you impose to help you decide when to obey someone in authority and when not to?

HONESTY

A recent study monitored 870 conversational statements by 130 people and found that only about one-third of the state-

* Quoted from Stanley Milgram's book, *Obedience to Authority,* New York: Harper & Row, 1974.

ments were completely honest. Other studies have found that it is impossible to divide children into groups of cheaters and non-cheaters. Almost all youngsters will cheat on tests under certain circumstances. Honesty, for most of us, is situational. We impose high standards on our children that we don't follow ourselves. Should we be so pragmatic about honesty—or is it an absolute value that transcends practical considerations?

What would you do in the following situations?

· You're 14 and small for your age. You're going to a movie theater that charges one dollar for children and three dollars for people over 12. Do you buy the child or adult ticket?
· You have just paid your restaurant check. You realize that the cashier gave you a five-dollar bill in your change instead of the one-dollar bill you should have received. Do you point out her error and give back the money?
· You have just been called by a TV rating service. You are watching Channel 2, but your father is a salesman at Channel 5, and his job is helped by high ratings. What do you say to the interviewer?
· A friend has been dieting strenuously for two months. She says to you, "Don't I look thinner?" You cannot see any difference in her figure. What do you say?
· While shopping in the supermarket you become very thirsty. You decide to buy a six-pack of juice and to drink one can now. You taste it and don't like it. Do you buy the six-pack anyway, do you offer to pay for the one you drank, or do you just put all the cans including the opened one on the nearest shelf?

My Last Lie: Everyone tells about the last lie she or he told, including "white" lies.

· What made you decide to lie instead of telling the truth?
· How did you feel about it? Comfortable? Uneasy?
· Could you have handled the situation in any other way?

CHEATING

What would you do if you entered a competition that you were convinced was so rigged that your only chance to win depended on your "bending the rules"?

Rank in order:

· withdraw from the contest and tell officials or newspaper reporters what is going on
· withdraw quietly, not tell anyone
· compete honestly in the belief that the activity itself is worth going out for, even though you know you can't win
· cheat just enough to give yourself a "fair" chance
· cheat as hard as you can

Which of these would be hardest for you?

· copy answers from someone else's test paper
· let someone copy from your paper
· be caught cheating by your teacher in front of the whole class
· have your parents find out about your cheating

Provocative Questions:

· Would you cheat on a test if you knew the grade was not going to be counted toward your grade for the term?
· Are there times when it is right to cheat?

23

RELIGION STRATEGIES

We often perform the same religious rituals that our parents did before us, without really thinking about what our religion means to us.

Lucky Thirteen (Strategy 13): List thirteen rituals connected with your religion. If you were limited in your practice of religion, which three would you give up first? Which three would you defy authority to continue?

My Favorite Things (Strategy 1): List ten things you love to do that have something to do with your religion. Make up codings.

Priorities (Strategy 5):
Which of these would be the worst for you?

· to have to go to church/temple in old clothes
· never to be able to attend religious services again
· to attend services every single Sabbath for the rest of your life

If you were going to marry a person of another religion, which do you think would be best for the children?

· to agree beforehand to bring them up in the religion of one of the parents and not have anything to do with the religious observances of the other
· to observe both religions, going first to one house of worship and then the other, and celebrate both sets of holidays

· to convert to a new religion and bring the children up in that
· not to have any religion at all

The Ten Commandments: These commandments are the basis for much of Judeo-Christian morality. As a religious person, do you feel it is important to obey all the commandments totally? If not, under what conditions would you or would you not obey each one? Questions like these can be dealt with by adapting the Values Spectrum (Strategy 6) to the Ten Commandments, as in these examples:

1. Thou shalt have no other gods before me.

DASHBOARD DICK	GODFEARING GUS
has 15 religious symbols on his dashboard, burns a fatted calf every morning, and then lights incense.	respects no authority but God —not police, parents, teachers, etc. Unless God tells him what to do, he won't do anything.

3. Thou shalt not take the name of the Lord thy God in vain.

PROFANE PATTY	RESPECTFUL ROSE
orders breakfast in a diner by saying, "Give me goddam juice, goddam eggs, goddam toast, goddam coffee—and hurry, goddammit!"	won't mention God's name in prayer and won't write it more completely than G-d, even in the holiest context.

6. Thou shalt not kill.

KILLER KURT	PACIFIST PAUL
goes out of his way to poison cats and dogs, shoot humming-birds, and favors using con-victed criminals as targets for rifle practice.	won't kill any living thing, even a disease-carrying mos-quito. Won't even gargle be-cause he doesn't want to kill germs.

The same approach can be used for the rest of the command-ments.

Provocative Questions:

· If you were going to convert to another religion, which one would you choose and why?
· When have you been close to a miracle?

- Who is the most religious person you have ever known and what was she or he like?
- What are some examples of when religion helped you?
- What more would you like your religion to do for you?
- What more could you do to live a holier life?

Values Telegrams (Strategy 39): Send two action telegrams and two validation telegrams to your clergyman, to one member of your congregation, and to God.

Unfinished Sentences: Make copies of the appropriate adults' or children's unfinished sentences for each family member. Hand them out and ask everyone to fill out the form by completing the sentences.

Sentences for Children:

- My religion is important to me because . . .
- I want to be { confirmed / bat/bar mitzvahed } because . . .
- I like being a member of my religious group because . . .
- The most important thing I learned this year in Sunday School is . . .
- I dream that . . .
- I wonder why . . .
- I want to promise that . . .

Sentences for Adults:

- My religion is important to me because . . .
- We belong to a church/synagogue because . . .
- I like being a member of my religious group because . . .
- The most important thing I want my children to learn in religious school is . . .
- I dream that . . .
- I wonder why . . .
- I make a commitment that . . .

After family members have filled out their forms, they write "Ah-hah!" statements, and share their statement and their answers.

24

LEISURE STRATEGIES

The way we spend our leisure hours says a lot about what we value. How much do we value the time? Do we plan it? Or do we just drift into whatever comes along—and then ask ourselves afterward, "Where did the time go?" Do we choose passive enjoyments or do we do things ourselves? Do we prefer to be alone or with other people? What interests do we pursue?

Time Diaries: All family members keep a diary for one week. Record the ways you spend the 24 hours of each day. At the end of the week, everyone codes his or her own diary as follows, and brings it to a family discussion.

R time you were required to spend at an activity (work, school, family obligation)
L leisure time
A time you spent alone
P time you spent with other people
Pl time you had planned ahead for (by buying tickets, planning to meet someone, etc.)
 ! time spent actively (playing a game, learning a new skill, etc.)
pa time spent as a spectator (TV, movie, ball game, etc.)
X a moment you wished you were doing something else

Write and share "Ah-hah!" statements and take turns talking for three to five minutes about your diaries. You may want to expand upon your "Ah-hahs!", discuss patterns in your lives, or talk about new insights received from keeping and coding the diaries.

Without moralizing, criticizing, or judging, ask each other questions like these:

· How do you feel about the way you used your time this week?
· Would you want to change anything about it?
· Were you surprised to find out how much or how little time you spent in any particular activity?
· Would you want to make a self-contract (see Strategy 28) to change the way you spend your time?
· What would you do with your time if you could have one extra hour every day?

Spending (Strategy 17): Turn to page 85 for ideas on discussing ways that family members spent recent blocks of leisure time.

VACATIONS

"What was the best vacation you ever took?" Think about this for a minute or two and take two or three minutes to describe what you loved about it.

Describe your ideal one-week vacation in three to five minutes.

"If you wanted to take a vacation but didn't have much money, what would you do?" The starter skips around the table, whip-style, for a brief answer from everyone. Then all participate in a general discussion, coming up with alternatives (like saving up for the vacation, taking on extra work, taking it vicariously by reading about a place, exploring different, low-cost vacations, etc.).

"If you were a travel agent planning a special vacation for you and a special friend, what would you plan?" This question is challenging for older children and adolescents: it involves thinking about the person you would like to vacation with, what that person's special interests and desires are, and how much you are willing to mesh your own with theirs.

"What were the high point and low point of your last vacation?" This question can help set the stage for a discussion on how the next vacation can be better (shorter car ride, more eating breaks, taking a friend along, etc.).

Sports Worksheet: Number from 1 to 14 on a sheet of paper. The starter reads the following statements, which family members respond to by writing Y (for Yes), N (for No), or M (for Maybe).

1. If I have fun, I don't care if I win or lose.
2. I like to play against myself; that way I always win.
3. I like to play against people better than I.
4. I like to play against people worse than I.
5. I like to play against people just as good as I.
6. It's no fun if you can't argue.
7. I like games that have a lot of luck.
8. I like games that are mostly skill.
9. I like to gamble.
10. I like violent sports.
11. I'll play only if I am first-string.
12. I'd rather watch than play.
13. I like individual sports.
14. I like team sports.

Explain why you answered the way you did.

Sports Situations: The starter presents these situations, and people tell how they would handle them.

1. You are the coach of a third-grade baseball team. In a close game, one of your players hits a fly ball toward first base and the opposing first-base player drops it. You hear some of the parents of your players cheer. What would you do?

2. You are the president of a major college. Several alumni come to see you to tell you they are unhappy with the basketball team, because all the players have long hair. These alumni feel the players are setting a bad example, and they say they will stop giving money to the college (as a group they have been donating $100,000 a year) unless you enforce a short hair rule for all athletes. What do you do?

3. You are the manager of a professional baseball team. Your general manager has just made a trade for the best player in the league. The player tells you he does not want to abide by the team rules. He feels he should not have to go to practice as long as he continues to play better than anyone else. What do you do?

TELEVISION

By the time the average child in our society has finished high school, she or he has spent 11,000 hours in the classroom and 15,000 hours watching television. Millions of children get their tastes in food, their desires for toys, their ideas about ideal family life, their attitudes toward appropriate sex roles, and their clues on resolving conflicts from television. It can be a teaching tool, a babysitter, or an addiction. Values Clarification can help you consider the part you want TV to play in your family life.

How We Deal with TV in Our House: Rank in order the following ways of regulating your children's viewing, according to how comfortable you would be with each one:

· Unlimited viewing: Children may watch as much TV as they want, even skipping meals, staying up as late as they want, and missing school.

· Unlimited viewing in leisure time: Children can watch as much TV as they want as long as they meet demands of school and homework, meals, household chores, sleep needs, and so forth.

- Budgeted viewing: A set number of hours is alloted for each day or week. Within these hours children may watch any show they want.
- Limited viewing: Children may watch TV evenings, weekend mornings, in inclement weather, or when they are sick. They may not watch weekdays, mornings, and sunny days.
- Specified shows: Parents determine which shows are acceptable (public TV, educational documentaries, specials) and which are not (scary adventures, cartoons, sex and violence). Children must clear all shows ahead of time with parents.
- No TV for children: It is viewed as an adult occupation.
- No TV in household: Family rents a set or goes to someone else's home for special events.
- No TV for anyone: No provisions are *ever* made for watching TV.

After everyone has set priorities, explore the pros and cons of all possibilities.

My Favorite TV Programs: List ten shows you like to watch. Code your lists:

P If you were invited to a party, you would go there instead of watching this show.

D If your parents offered to take you out to dinner at your favorite restaurant, you would go instead of watching the show.

5 You think this is a good show for children under 5.

A You think you'll still like it when you're an adult.

V It has a lot of violence.

F It's funny.

R It provides a realistic view of people and situations in real life.

L You learn something of value from it.

T You would be proud to tell your teacher you watch it.

Follow up the coding with an "Ah-hah!" statement.

TV Toys: Rank in order these methods for deciding which TV-advertised toys to buy:

- whatever the children ask for
- they have to see the toy in action, either at the store or at a friend's house
- they have to pay half, either from allowance or doing special jobs
- they have to give three reasons why they want it
- they can't buy anything advertised on TV

Broken TV Set: Write down ten things you would do during the time you now watch TV if the TV set broke. Compare the activities with TV. Which do you get the most out of? Code the lists or use them as a discussion base.

25

MONEY STRATEGIES

Every year the McGuire children go to two county fairs. Before the first, they receive money to cover both. If they spend all the money on Fair No. 1, they will have none for Fair No. 2. Similarly, if all the money goes for food, there will be none for games or rides, and vice versa.

The children's parents make one round of the fairgrounds with them to look at all the places where they might spend their money: the booths selling ice cream and cotton candy, the ball-toss games, the rides, the souvenir stands. On this first walk, no money is spent. After the youngsters have looked at all the alternatives, they are free to spend their money as they wish.

This way of helping children learn how to handle money is a graphic use of alternatives, cherishing, and setting priorities. It demonstrates a nice balance between letting children make their own decisions and telling them what to do. Many situations can be handled this way, with parents setting the parameters and offering guidance but with the final decision left to the children.

Money enters into many family values decisions. Most of us have conflicting feelings about it. We want to have enough to live comfortably, enjoy life, and do what we want. Yet few of us like to think of ourselves as over-valuing it. How can we reconcile our needs and our desires for what money can bring with our wishes not to let the search for it dominate our lives? One way is through Values Clarification, and strategies like these.

Priorities (Strategy 5):

If your family won the $50,000 lottery, what would you do with the money? Rank in order:

· buy a house
· take the family on a trip around the world
· save for the children's college educations

If you needed more money than you were getting from your allowance, which would you be most likely to do?

· ask for a bigger allowance
· go without lunches
· take change from your mother's pocketbook
· get a paper route

If you were given a dollar a day to spend on some personal treat, what would you buy every day? Rank in order:

· ice cream
· cigarettes
· soda
· chewing gum
· magazines

Spending (Strategy 17): Everyone thinks about how she or he spent the last ten dollars (or five or two, for younger children), in terms of the following:

· Was it something you needed or just wanted?
· Are you glad you spent your money this way?
· Would you make the same decision again? If not, what would you do differently?

Money Diary: Everyone in the family keeps a money diary, writing down all expenditures. At the end of a month, total up the various categories: clothes, movies, food, etc. People share their answers to these questions:

· Do any of the totals surprise you?
· Do you feel you've gotten your money's worth in each category?

· How might you do things differently next month?

Poverty Modules (for families whose children are at least school-age): Many children in our affluent society have no notion of what poverty is. They cannot envision its hardships. No amount of telling them can make them truly understand what millions of people go through. There *are* ways to help them experience the implications of poverty, though, on a limited and temporary basis, by duplicating or "acting out" situations only too real to many low-income families.

You can all agree to turn off the heat in your house some cold winter night and leave it off for twenty-four hours. As the family finds its activities curtailed and tempers shortened, discuss the way poverty shapes people's personalities.

You can live for one week on the money a welfare family would receive. Check with your local office to find out the amount.

Go to the Salvation Army or Goodwill Industries store in your town and try to find suitable school clothes for everyone in your family on that same welfare budget. Discuss what it feels like to wear other people's hand-me-downs. Would it be different if you knew they were from someone very rich? Or if they had belonged to someone who had died?

Budgeting: Encourage your child to use money wisely by:

· Giving a child a turn at buying the week's groceries, staying within a certain sum.
· Giving a child a yearly clothing allowance, within which she or he has freedom to buy what she or he wants.

Money Whips: Each person names two things she or he could do personally to help the family save money. The after-whip discussion might range from the purpose of saving it (necessity, or the desire to save for some luxury), to the different amounts of money family members spend for different purposes, to the importance of money in our lives.

Everyone answers the question, "If someone gave you a million dollars, how much of it would you keep for yourself?" The discussion then considers what people would do with the rest;

whether they would give any to charity, and if so, which one; and what they would do with the part that they kept.

Provocative Questions (Strategy 8): Should people get paid for doing housework in their own home? If a father works outside the home and the mother does the housework, how much of his salary should she get for her work? Should children be paid for making their beds, doing dishes, taking out the garbage? Should older children be paid for babysitting with younger ones?

What's the purpose of an allowance? Should children be able to spend their allowance money on anything they want? Candy, gum, soda, comic books? Should they be required to save any of it? Should they be punished by having it withheld? What kinds of things should be covered—movies, swimming, lunch, bus fare, clothing, shoe repair? What's a fair allowance in your neighborhood, with your style of life? Should it be the same for all the children in a family?

Advertising in My Life: Few of us realize how many of our spending choices are influenced by advertising. Anyone growing up in our society has to learn how to deal with it. Everyone notes "Ten Things I'd Like to Own." Paste cut-out pictures from newspaper or magazine ads, or make drawings and write out slogans from TV commercials. Code your list as follows:

$ you can afford to buy the item right now
N you need it
S someone you know well has one
 i people would think you were more important if you had one
A your parents would approve of your having one
D your parents would disapprove
 * the 3 items that you want the most

After coding, everyone makes one "Ah-hah!" statement. The children in one family, for example, said things like: "The things I want most wouldn't make me seem more important," "My parents would approve of everything on my list," and "I can't afford any of the things on my list."

The discussion that follows might deal with questions such as:

How realistic are your wants? How much are you influenced by your friends? How much by the advertising itself?

Give! Every day we are asked to contribute money to a wide variety of special-interest groups. Most of these organizations have worthwhile goals, many of which are in line with our own values. But it is impossible for one person to support all of them. How, then, do we decide how to allot our charitable donations? This strategy can help us make these decisions.

Everyone ranks in order of importance these concerns:

· health
· peace
· poverty
· environment
· religion
· political party
· feminism
· minority-group rights
· culture (art, music, etc.)
· other (one you're especially interested in)

Write down next to each one the approximate amount of money you gave to this kind of group in the past year.

· Do the amounts you gave reflect your rankings?
· What percentage of your income/allowance do you give to charity or social action causes?
· What percentage do you think you should give? (The traditional church tithe has been 10 percent of total income; the Internal Revenue Service allows taxpayers to deduct charitable deductions of 20 to 50 percent of their adjusted gross income.)
· Do you want to change your contributions as a result of your answers to any of these questions?

More than Money: List five things you value more than money. Then test your values by asking and answering questions like these:

For those who said "Health":

- For adults: Would you spend extra to have an electrocardio-gram included in your yearly physical exam?
- For children: Would you have a yearly physical exam if you had to pay for it out of your allowance?

For those who said "Friends":

- How much money would you lend a friend without asking what she or he needed it for?

For those who said "Love":

- What would you give up in order to give your loved one a gift that you know she/he is yearning for?

26

WORK AND SCHOOL STRATEGIES

For most of us over the age of 6, the bulk of our waking hours are spent at work—either on a job, in the home, or at school. The lucky ones among us love their work, eagerly look forward to it, and find it fulfilling. But many other people just get through their work obligations in order to get on with their real lives. Becoming clearer about our values helps us get more from our working lives. We are in a better position to do what we like and like what we do.

Priorities (Strategy 5):
Which of these jobs would you like best?

- pickle inspector in a factory, eight hours a day pulling imperfect pickles off the conveyor belt
- toll collector on a thruway
- wiper at the local car wash

Which of these chores do you like the least?

- emptying the garbage
- vacuuming
- washing greasy pots and pans

Which do you most like to do?

- write papers in English
- take math tests
- do science projects

Lucky Thirteen (Strategy 13): List thirteen tasks you do at school. Draw a line through the three you like the least. Circle the three that are the most enjoyable part of your day. How can you make the less appealing tasks more interesting?

List thirteen jobs held by people you know. Draw a line through the three you would least want to hold yourself. Circle the three that seem the most rewarding. Give reasons for your choices. Add to the list a job that you think you would like to hold, if it is not already on it.

List thirteen household chores you do either regularly or occasionally. If you could get someone else to do three, which would you get rid of? Draw a line through them. Circle the three you get most gratification from. Is there some way you can make the others more gratifying? Can you think of an alternative way of dividing the household work?

My Favorite Things (Strategy 1): Everyone makes a list of "Ten Things I Love to Do" either at school or work. Code the list:

D I do it every day
O I'd like to do it more often
L I learn something new when I do it
I It makes me feel important to do it
P I do it with other people
M I would miss doing this if it were not part of my day

Write an "Ah-hah!" statement about what you have learned about yourself and your work.

My Least Favorite Things: Everyone lists "Ten Things I Don't Like to Do" at school or work. Code the list:

D I do it every day
S Someone else would and could do it if I asked
I I feel inadequate when I do it
P I do it with other people
A I do it alone

Everyone brainstorms about everyone else's list, to try to figure out ways to make these tasks more appealing or to eliminate them from the regular routine.

Dreams Can Come True (Strategy 10): Everyone gets two minutes to talk about the perfect school, job, teacher, or boss. The discussion then focuses on how each family member can make reality come closer to his or her dream.

Classified Ad (Strategy 34): Write a "Situation Wanted" ad for yourself. If anyone needs to earn extra money or is really interested in changing jobs, actually place it in the appropriate paper—the local paper for the kids, the right trade or big-city paper for the grown-ups.

Values Spectrum (Strategy 6):

WORKAHOLIC WANDA . . . works 365 days a year, 14 hours a day, takes time out only to eat and sleep. Never takes a vacation or spends time with the family.

LAZY LOLA faints when anyone mentions the possibility of her taking a job. That would mean she couldn't sleep till noon every day and play all day and night.

SLAVEDRIVER SYLVESTER . . makes his children work from dawn to dark while he lies on the couch watching TV.

LENIENT LENNY pushes his healthy children in wheelchairs so they won't have to exert themselves to walk.

27

LOVE AND SEXUALITY STRATEGIES

Moral codes were once so strict that decisions about love and sexuality were often taken out of the hands of youth. Young boys and girls were not allowed to be together unchaperoned. Fear of pregnancy and of societal penalties for early sexual activity led many young people to abide by their elders' expectations. Today, reliable birth control and a more accepting attitude about sex have blurred behavioral guidelines. Adults, too, are often unclear about their standards.

Young people today have to assume more responsibility for their own actions. Many base their decisions on what their friends are doing, on what they've seen in the movies, or on an impulse of the moment. But they can be encouraged to think about what alternatives are available to them in handling sexual and love relationships, what the consequences are of the various alternatives, and how they can decide what is best for them.

People need to know that they are not at the mercy of other people or momentary circumstances, but that they have real choices about the way they will lead their lives. This is as true for sexuality as it is for any other aspect of life. With this attitude, young people can feel—and indeed can be—more in control of their own lives. And they can gradually assume more and more responsibility for making their own decisions.

The Meaning of Love: Everyone writes out a definition of love. Then everyone writes down the following list of loving relationships:

- sweetheart
- parent/child
- sister/brother
- pet

- husband/wife
- best friend
- grandparent/grandchild
- other

Put a check next to those relationships to which your definition of love applies. If you want to, rewrite your definition. Share your definitions.

Classified Ad (Strategy 34):

1. Write a "Spouse Wanted" ad. What characteristics would you want applicants to have in terms of age, income, education, appearance, personality, attitudes, values, etc.?
2. Write a "Spouse Available" ad, offering yourself in marriage. What could you offer someone?

Priorities (Strategy 5):
Rank these reasons for getting married:

- having someone to be with so you won't be alone
- having a sexual partner
- having and raising children
- forming an economic partnership
- having fun together
- knowing that one person understands you better than anyone else in the world

You are a 15-year-old boy sitting with your 14-year-old girl friend in her home. Just sitting next to her gets you sexually aroused. What do you do?

- kiss her goodnight and go home and masturbate
- neck and pet with her and ask her to masturbate you
- have sexual intercourse
- suggest that the two of you do something active like going for a walk or a bike ride

You are the parents of a 19-year-old girl who has just brought her boyfriend home for a weekend. You know they have been sleeping together at college. Rank in order the sleeping arrangements you would feel most comfortable with in your home:

- they sleep in the same room (you accept their relationship)
- they sleep in adjoining rooms (you go to sleep early and say nothing to either one)
- their bedrooms are separated by two floors (you stay up all night to be sure they don't get together)
- they sleep in separate rooms (you tell your daughter she can do what she wants when she is away, but in your home you don't approve of sexual activity between young unmarried people)

You are a pregnant unmarried 16-year-old girl. What should you do? Rank these possibilities in order:

- have the baby and bring it up yourself
- have the baby and give it up for adoption
- get married and have the baby
- have the baby and let a relative (mother, sister, cousin, aunt) raise it
- have an abortion

Rank these items according to their importance in a good marriage:

- enjoying the same kind of leisure-time activities
- agreeing on how to raise the children
- having enough money to live on comfortably
- having a wide circle of friends you both enjoy
- being able to let each other know when you are angry
- being able to ask for what you want
- having a good sexual relationship

Expectations of Marriage:

1. For young people: Imagine it is 10/15/20 years from now. You are married. In your diary you are recording the events and feelings of the past weekend. With this diary entry show what you think marriage will be like. Read what you have written. Is this what you hope your marriage will be like?

2. For married people: Think back to the day before you got married. If you had confided to a diary that day your hopes and expectations of marriage, what would you have written? Think about how your own marriage has fitted in with those ideas. How has it differed? Are you pleased or disappointed? What can you do to make your marriage come closer to your ideal?

This exercise can bring husband and wife, and parents and children closer together as you all share some of your feelings about this basic human relationship.

Values Spectrum (Strategy 6).

FREE FRAN . . . . . . has absolute freedom to be sexually active whenever and with whomever she wants. Her parents encourage her to go to bed with a boy as easily as she would say hello to him.

RESTRICTED RITA is not allowed to see any boys at all. She goes to an all-girls school, has to come right home after school, isn't even allowed to speak to a boy on the phone.

For young people: Where are you on this spectrum?
Where would you like to be?
If you were a parent, where would your teenagers be?

For parents: Where were you on this spectrum when you were the age of your children?
Where are your children?
Where would you like them to be?

CONTRACEPTIVE CARL . . . gave his daughter birth-control pills when she had her first menstrual period and watches her to be sure she takes her pill every day.

IGNORANT IRVING doesn't want his children to find out about birth control till after they're married. He won't let them read books or attend school lectures and won't answer their questions.

FAITHFUL FLO . . . . .

has never had a sexual relationship with anyone besides her husband, even though he walked out on her 20 years ago, because she considers the sacrament of marriage sacred. "Even though my husband may not care about me any more, I still take my marriage vows seriously," she says.

ADULTEROUS ADELE

has had many sexual affairs since her marriage because she considers monogamy outdated. "Being faithful to one man is like eating the same thing for dinner every night of my life," she says.

EPILOGUE

All of us who are trying to perform that incredibly complex job of bringing up children realize that whatever we do or don't do will have an impact on them. Most parents accept this awesome responsibility as one that goes with the territory. We may not be prepared for it ahead of time, but when we are actually face to face with it, we don't run away. We stay, we cope, we try. Oh how we try! Ultimately, the trying boils down to values. Which is what this book has been all about.

When the crunch is on, how do *your* values affect the way you raise your children? What do you support? What do you discourage? What do you allow? What do you refuse? How do you help them as they struggle to find *their* values?

With this book we have tried to give you and your whole family some experiences to go through to find out what your true values are and how to live by them. They have been forged from our own life experiences and from many years of working with people on the arduous but exciting process of clarifying values.

Some people leave their children money, property, or other material goods. We want to leave ours a much more valuable legacy—a collection of tools for finding the values to guide them throughout life. With these tools, they will build lives in which they know what they value and value what they know. Come, let us search and build together.

Alphabetical Listing of Strategies

Catalog

If you are interested in a list of fine Paperback
books, covering a wide range of subjects
and interests, send your name and address,
requesting your free catalog, to:

McGraw-Hill Paperbacks
1221 Avenue of Americas
New York, N.Y. 10020